THE PIGEON

A FANTASY IN THREE ACTS

BY

JOHN GALSWORTHY

"... Without that, Monsieur, all is
dry as a parched skin of orange."

NEW YORK

CHARLES SCRIBNER'S SONS

1913

PLAYS BY
JOHN GALSWORTHY

———

THE SILVER BOX
JOY
STRIFE
JUSTICE
THE LITTLE DREAM
THE ELDEST SON
THE PIGEON

THE PIGEON

A FANTASY IN THREE ACTS

PERSONS OF THE PLAY

CHRISTOPHER WELLWYN, *an artist*
ANN, *his daughter*
GUINEVERE MEGAN, *a flower-seller*
RORY MEGAN, *her husband*
FERRAND, *an alien*
TIMSON, *once a cabman*
EDWARD BERTLEY, *a Canon*
ALFRED CALWAY, *a Professor*
SIR THOMAS HOXTON, *a Justice of the Peace*
*Also a police constable, three humble-men, and some
    curious persons*

*The action passes in Wellwyn's Studio, and the street out-
side.*

CAST OF THE FIRST PRODUCTION

BY

MESSRS. J. E. VEDRENNE AND DENNIS EADIE

AT THE

ROYALTY THEATRE, LONDON, ON JANUARY 30TH, 1912

CHRISTOPHER WELLWYN	MR. WHITFORD KANE
ANN	MISS GLADYS COOPER
FERRAND	MR. DENNIS EADIE
TIMSON	MR. WILFRED SHINE
MRS. MEGAN	MISS MARGARET MORRIS
MEGAN	MR. STANLEY LOGAN
CANON BERTLEY	MR. HUBERT HARBEN
PROFESSOR CALWAY	MR. FRANK VERNON
SIR THOMAS HOXTON	MR. FREDERICK LLOYD
POLICE CONSTABLE	MR. ARTHUR B. MURRAY
FIRST HUMBLE-MAN	MR. W. LEMMON WARDE
SECOND HUMBLE-MAN	MR. F. B. J. SHARP
THIRD HUMBLE-MAN	MR. ARTHUR BOWYER
A LOAFER	MR. ARTHUR BAXENDELL

ACT I

It is the night of Christmas Eve, the SCENE *is a Studio,
flush with the street, having a skylight darkened by a
fall of snow. There is no one in the room, the walls
of which are whitewashed, above a floor of bare dark
boards. A fire is cheerfully burning. On a model's
platform stands an easel and canvas. There are
busts and pictures; a screen, a little stool, two arm-
chairs, and a long old-fashioned settle under the window. A door in one wall leads to the house, a door
in the opposite wall to the model's dressing-room, and
the street door is in the centre of the wall between.
On a low table a Russian samovar is hissing, and
beside it on a tray stands a teapot, with glasses,
lemon, sugar, and a decanter of rum. Through a
huge uncurtained window close to the street door the
snowy lamplit street can be seen, and beyond it the
river and a night of stars.*

*The sound of a latchkey turned in the lock of the street
door, and* ANN WELLWYN *enters, a girl of seventeen,
with hair tied in a ribbon and covered by a scarf.
Leaving the door open, she turns up the electric light
and goes to the fire. She throws off her scarf and
long red cloak. She is dressed in a high evening
frock of some soft white material. Her movements*

1

are quick and substantial.   Her face, full of no non-
sense, is decided and sincere, with deep-set eyes, and
a capable, well-shaped forehead.   Shredding off her
gloves she warms her hands.

In the doorway appear the figures of two men.   The first
is rather short and slight, with a soft short beard,
bright soft eyes, and a crumply face.   Under his
squash hat his hair is rather plentiful and rather
grey.   He wears an old brown ulster and woollen
gloves, and is puffing at a hand-made cigarette.   He
is ANN's *father,* WELLWYN, *the artist.   His com-*
panion is a well-wrapped clergyman of medium
height and stoutish build, with a pleasant, rosy face,
rather shining eyes, and rather chubby clean-shaped
lips; in appearance, indeed, a grown-up boy.   He
*is the Vicar of the parish—*CANON BERTLEY.

BERTLEY. My dear Wellwyn, the whole question of
reform is full of difficulty.   When you have two men
like Professor Calway and Sir Thomas Hoxton taking
diametrically opposite points of view, as we've seen
to-night, I confess, I——

WELLWYN. Come in, Vicar, and have some grog.

BERTLEY. Not to-night, thanks!   Christmas to-
morrow!   Great temptation, though, this room!   Good-
night, Wellwyn;   good-night, Ann!

ANN. [*Coming from the fire towards the tea-table.*]
Good-night, Canon Bertley.

> [*He goes out, and* WELLWYN, *shutting the door*
> *after him, approaches the fire.*

ANN. [*Sitting on the little stool, with her back to the fire, and making tea.*] Daddy!

WELLWYN. My dear?

ANN. You say you liked Professor Calway's lecture. Is it going to do you any good, that's the question?

WELLWYN. I—I hope so, Ann.

ANN. I took you on purpose. Your charity's getting simply awful. Those two this morning cleared out all my housekeeping money.

WELLWYN. Um! Um! I quite understand your feeling.

ANN. They both had your card, so I couldn't refuse —didn't know what you'd said to them. Why don't you make it a rule never to give your card to anyone except really decent people, and—picture dealers, of course.

WELLWYN. My dear, I have—often.

ANN. Then why don't you keep it? It's a frightful habit. You *are* naughty, Daddy. One of these days you'll get yourself into most fearful complications.

WELLWYN. My dear, when they—when they look at you?

ANN. You know the house wants all sorts of things. Why do you speak to them at all?

WELLWYN. I don't—they speak to me.

> [*He takes off his ulster and hangs it over the back
> of an arm-chair.*

ANN. They see you coming. Anybody can see *you* coming, Daddy. That's why you ought to be so careful. I shall make you wear a hard hat. Those squashy hats of yours are hopelessly inefficient.

WELLWYN. [*Gazing at his hat.*] Calway wears one.

ANN. As if anyone would beg of Professor Calway.

WELLWYN. Well—perhaps not. You know, Ann, I admire that fellow. Wonderful power of—of—theory! How a man can be so absolutely tidy in his mind! It's most exciting.

ANN. Has any one begged of you to-day?

WELLWYN. [*Doubtfully.*] No—no.

ANN. [*After a long, severe look.*] Will you have rum in your tea?

WELLWYN. [*Crestfallen.*] Yes, my dear—a good deal.

ANN. [*Pouring out the rum, and handing him the glass.*] Well, who was it?

WELLWYN. He didn't beg of me. [*Losing himself in recollection.*] Interesting old creature, Ann—real type. Old cabman.

ANN. Where?

WELLWYN. Just on the Embankment.

ANN. Of course! Daddy, you know the Embankment ones are *always* rotters.

WELLWYN. Yes, my dear; but this wasn't.

ANN. Did you give him your card?

WELLWYN. I—I—don't——

ANN. *Did* you, Daddy?

WELLWYN. I'm rather afraid I may have!

ANN. May have! It's simply immoral.

WELLWYN. Well, the old fellow was so awfully hu-

man, Ann. Besides, I didn't give him any money—
hadn't got any.

ANN. Look here, Daddy! Did you ever ask anybody for anything? You know you never did, you'd
starve first. So would anybody decent. Then, why
won't you see that people who beg are rotters?

WELLWYN. But, my dear, we're not all the same. They
wouldn't do it if it wasn't natural to them. One likes to
be friendly. What's the use of being alive if one isn't?

ANN. Daddy, you're hopeless.

WELLWYN. But, look here, Ann, the whole thing's so
jolly complicated. According to Calway, we're to give
the State all we can spare, to make the undeserving
deserving. He's a Professor; he ought to know. But
old Hoxton's always dinning it into me that we ought
to support private organisations for helping the deserving, and damn the undeserving. Well, that's just the
opposite. And he's a J.P. Tremendous experience.
And the Vicar seems to be for a little bit of both. Well,
what the devil—? My trouble is, whichever I'm with,
he always converts me. [*Ruefully.*] And there's no fun
in any of them.

ANN. [*Rising.*] Oh! Daddy, you are so—don't you
know that you're the despair of all social reformers?
[*She envelops him.*] There's a tear in the left knee of
your trousers. You're not to wear them again.

WELLWYN. Am I likely to?

ANN. I shouldn't be a bit surprised if it isn't your
only pair. D'you know what I live in terror of?

[WELLWYN *gives her a queer and apprehensive look.*

ANN. That you'll take them off some day, and give
them away in the street. Have you got any money?
[*She feels in his coat, and he is his trousers—they find
nothing.*] Do you know that your pockets are one enor-
mous hole?

WELLWYN. No!

ANN. Spiritually.

WELLWYN. Oh! Ah! H'm!

ANN. [*Severely.*] Now, look here, Daddy! [*She takes
him by his lappels.*] Don't imagine that it isn't the most
disgusting luxury on your part to go on giving away
things as you do! You know what you really are, I
suppose—a sickly sentimentalist!

WELLWYN. [*Breaking away from her, disturbed.*] It
isn't sentiment. It's simply that they seem to me
so—so—jolly. If I'm to give up feeling sort of
—nice in here [*he touches his chest*] about people—it
doesn't matter *who* they are—then I don't know
what I'm to do. I shall have to sit with my head
in a bag.

ANN. I think you ought to.

WELLWYN. I suppose they see I like them—then
they tell me things. After that, of course you can't
help doing what you can.

ANN. Well, if you *will* love them up!

WELLWYN. My dear, I don't want to. It isn't *them*
especially—why, I feel it even with old Calway sometimes. It's only Providence that he doesn't want anything of me—except to make me like himself—con-
found him!

ANN. [*Moving towards the door into the house—impressively.*] What you don't see is that other people aren't a bit like *you*.

WELLWYN. Well, thank God!

ANN. It's so old-fashioned too! I'm going to bed—I just leave you to your conscience.

WELLWYN. Oh!

ANN. [*Opening the door—severely.*] Good-night—[*with a certain weakening*] you old—Daddy!

> [*She jumps at him, gives him a hug, and goes out.*
>
> [WELLWYN *stands perfectly still. He first gazes up at the skylight, then down at the floor. Slowly he begins to shake his head, and mutter, as he moves towards the fire.*

WELLWYN. Bad lot. . . . Low type—no backbone, no stability!

> [*There comes a fluttering knock on the outer door. As the sound slowly enters his consciousness, he begins to wince, as though he knew, but would not admit its significance. Then he sits down, covering his ears. The knocking does not cease.* WELLWYN *drops first one, then both hands, rises, and begins to sidle towards the door. The knocking becomes louder.*

WELLWYN. Ah dear! Tt! Tt! Tt!

> [*After a look in the direction of* ANN's *disappearance, he opens the street door a very little way. By the light of the lamp there can be seen a young girl in dark clothes, huddled in a shawl to which*

the snow is clinging.   She has on her arm a bas-
ket covered with a bit of sacking.

WELLWYN. I can't, you know; it's impossible.

[*The girl says nothing, but looks at him with dark
eyes.*

WELLWYN. [*Wincing.*] Let's see—I don't know you
—do I?

[*The girl, speaking in a soft, hoarse voice, with a
faint accent of reproach:* "Mrs. Megan—you
give me this—" *She holds out a dirty visiting
card.*

WELLWYN. [*Recoiling from the card.*] Oh! Did I?
Ah! When?

MRS. MEGAN. You 'ad some vi'lets off of me larst
spring.   You give me 'arf a crown.

[*A smile tries to visit her face.*

WELLWYN. [*Looking stealthily round.*] Ah! Well,
come in—just for a minute—it's very cold—and tell us
what it is.

[*She comes in stolidly, a sphinx-like figure, with
her pretty tragic little face.*

WELLWYN. I don't remember you. [*Looking closer.*]
Yes, *I do.*   Only—you weren't the same—were you?

MRS. MEGAN. [*Dully.*] I seen trouble since.

WELLWYN. Trouble! Have some tea?

[*He looks anxiously at the door into the house, then
goes quickly to the table, and pours out a glass of
tea, putting rum into it.*

WELLWYN. [*Handing her the tea.*] Keeps the cold out!
Drink it off!

[MRS. MEGAN *drinks it off, chokes a little, and
almost immediately seems to get a size larger.*
WELLWYN *watches her with his head held on
one side, and a smile broadening on his face.*

WELLWYN. Cure for all evils, um?

MRS. MEGAN. It warms you.　　　　　[*She smiles.*

WELLWYN. [*Smiling back, and catching himself out.*]
Well! You know, I oughtn't.

MRS. MEGAN. [*Conscious of the disruption of his per-
sonality, and withdrawing into her tragic abyss.*] I
wouldn't 'a come, but you told me if I wanted an
'and——

WELLWYN. [*Gradually losing himself in his own na-
ture.*] Let me see—corner of Flight Street, wasn't it?

MRS. MEGAN. [*With faint eagerness.*] Yes, sir, an'
I told you about me vi'lets—it was a luvly spring
day.

WELLWYN. Beautiful! Beautiful! Birds singing,
and the trees, &c.! We had quite a talk. You had a
baby with you.

MRS. MEGAN. Yes. I got married since then.

WELLWYN. Oh! Ah! Yes! [*Cheerfully.*] And how's
the baby?

MRS. MEGAN. [*Turning to stone.*] I lost her.

WELLWYN. Oh! poor— Um!

MRS. MEGAN. [*Impassive.*] You　said　something
abaht makin' a picture of me. [*With faint eagerness.*]
So I thought I might come, in case you'd forgotten.

WELLWYN. [*Looking at her intently.*] Things going
badly?

MRS. MEGAN. [*Stripping the sacking off her basket.*] I keep 'em covered up, but the cold gets to 'em. Thruppence—that's all I've took.

WELLWYN. Ho! Tt! Tt! [*He looks into the basket.*] Christmas, too!

MRS. MEGAN. They're dead.

WELLWYN. [*Drawing in his breath.*] Got a *good* husband?

MRS. MEGAN. He plays cards.

WELLWYN. Oh, Lord! And what are you doing out —with a cold like that? [*He taps his chest.*

MRS. MEGAN. We was sold up this morning—he's gone off with 'is mates. Haven't took enough yet for a night's lodgin'.

WELLWYN. [*Correcting a spasmodic dive into his pockets.*] But who buys *flowers* at this time of night?

[MRS. MEGAN *looks at him, and faintly smiles.*

WELLWYN. [*Rumpling his hair.*] Saints above us! Here! Come to the fire!

[*She follows him to the fire. He shuts the street door.*

WELLWYN. Are your feet wet? [*She nods.*] Well, sit down here, and take them off. That's right.

[*She sits on the stool. And after a slow look up at him, which has in it a deeper knowledge than belongs of right to her years, begins taking off her shoes and stockings.* WELLWYN *goes to the door into the house, opens it, and listens with a sort of stealthy casualness. He returns whistling, but not out loud. The girl has finished tak-*

*ing off her stockings, and turned her bare toes
to the flames. She shuffles them back under her
skirt.*

WELLWYN. How old are you, my child?

MRS. MEGAN. Nineteen, come Candlemas.

WELLWYN. And what's your name?

MRS. MEGAN. Guinevere.

WELLWYN. What? Welsh?

MRS. MEGAN. Yes—from Battersea.

WELLWYN. And your husband?

MRS. MEGAN. No. Irish, 'e is. Notting Dale, 'e
comes from.

WELLWYN. Roman Catholic?

MRS. MEGAN. Yes. My 'usband's an atheist as
well.

WELLWYN. I see. [*Abstractedly.*] How jolly! And
how old is he—this young man of yours?

MRS. MEGAN. 'E'll be twenty soon.

WELLWYN. Babes in the wood! Does he treat you
badly?

MRS. MEGAN. No.

WELLWYN. Nor drink?

MRS. MEGAN. No. He's not a bad one. Only he
gets playin' cards—then 'e'll fly the kite.

WELLWYN. I see. And when he's not flying it, what
does he do?

MRS. MEGAN. [*Touching her basket.*] Same as me.
Other jobs tires 'im.

WELLWYN. That's very nice! [*He checks himself.*]
Well, what am I to do with you?

MRS. MEGAN. Of course, I could get me night's lodging if I like to do—the same as some of them.

WELLWYN. No! no! Never, my child! Never!

MRS. MEGAN. It's easy that way.

WELLWYN. Heavens! But your husband! Um?

MRS. MEGAN. [*With stoical vindictiveness.*] He's after one I know of.

WELLWYN. Tt! What a pickle!

MRS. MEGAN. I'll 'ave to walk about the streets.

WELLWYN. [*To himself.*] Now how can I?

> [MRS. MEGAN *looks up and smiles at him, as if she had already discovered that he is peculiar.*

WELLWYN. You see, the fact is, I mustn't give you anything—because—well, for one-thing I haven't got it. There are other reasons, but that's the—real one. But, now, there's a little room where my models dress. I wonder if you could sleep there. Come, and see.

> [*The Girl gets up lingeringly, loth to leave the warmth. She takes up her wet stockings.*

MRS. MEGAN. Shall I put them on again?

WELLWYN. No, no; there's a nice warm pair of slippers. [*Seeing the steam rising from her.*] Why, you're wet all over. Here, wait a little!

> [*He crosses to the door into the house, and after stealthy listening, steps through. The Girl, like a cat, steals back to the warmth of the fire.* WELLWYN *returns with a candle, a canary-coloured bath gown, and two blankets.*

WELLWYN. Now then! [*He precedes her towards the door of the model's room.*] Hsssh! [*He opens the door and

holds up the candle to show her the room.] Will it do?
There's a couch. You'll find some washing things.
Make yourself quite at home. See!

> [*The Girl, perfectly dumb, passes through with her*
> *basket—and her shoes and stockings.* WELLWYN
> *hands her the candle, blankets, and bath gown.*

WELLWYN. Have a good sleep, child! Forget that
you're alive! [*He closes the door, mournfully.*] Done it
again! [*He goes to the table, cuts a large slice of cake,
knocks on the door, and hands it in.*] Chow-chow!
[*Then, as he walks away, he sights the opposite door.*]
Well—damn it, what *could* I have done? Not a far-
thing on me! [*He goes to the street door to shut it, but first
opens it wide to confirm himself in his hospitality.*] Night
like this!

> [*A sputter of snow is blown in his face. A voice*
> *says:* "Monsieur, pardon!" WELLWYN *re-*
> *coils spasmodically. A figure moves from the*
> *lamp-post to the doorway. He is seen to be*
> *young and to have ragged clothes. He speaks*
> *again:* "You do not remember me, Monsieur?
> My name is Ferrand—it was in Paris, in
> the Champs-Elysées—by the fountain. . . .
> When you came to the door, Monsieur—I am
> not made of iron. . . . Tenez, here is your
> card—I have never lost it." *He holds out to*
> WELLWYN *an old and dirty visiting card. As*
> *inch by inch he has advanced into the doorway,*
> *the light from within falls on him, a tall gaunt*
> *young pagan with fair hair and reddish golden*

*stubble of beard, a long ironical nose a little to one
side, and large, grey, rather prominent eyes.
There is a certain grace in his figure and movements; his clothes are nearly dropping off him.*

WELLWYN. [*Yielding to a pleasant memory.*] Ah! yes.
By the fountain. I was sitting there, and you came
and ate a roll, and drank the water.

FERRAND. [*With faint eagerness.*] My breakfast. I
was in poverty—veree bad off. You gave me ten francs.
I thought I had a little the right [WELLWYN *makes a
movement of disconcertion*], seeing you said that if I came
to England——

WELLWYN. Um! And so you've come?

FERRAND. It was time that I consolidated my for-
tunes, Monsieur.

WELLWYN. And you—have——

[*He stops embarrassed.*

FERRAND. [*Shrugging his ragged shoulders.*] One is
not yet Rothschild.

WELLWYN. [*Sympathetically.*] No. [*Yielding to memory.*] We talked philosophy.

FERRAND. I have not yet changed my opinion. We
other vagabonds, we are exploited by the bourgeois.
This is always my idea, Monsieur.

WELLWYN. Yes—not quite the general view, perhaps! Well— [*Heartily.*] Come in! Very glad to see
you again.

FERRAND. [*Brushing his arms over his eyes.*] Pardon,
Monsieur—your goodness—I am a little weak. [*He
opens his coat, and shows a belt drawn very tight over his*

ragged shirt.] I tighten him one hole for each meal, during two days now. That gives you courage.

WELLWYN. [*With cooing sounds, pouring out tea, and adding rum.*] Have some of this. It'll buck you up.
[*He watches the young man drink.*

FERRAND. [*Becoming a size larger.*] Sometimes I think that I will never succeed to dominate my life, Monsieur—though I have no vices, except that I guard always the aspiration to achieve success. But I will not roll myself under the machine of existence to gain a nothing every day. I must find with what to fly a little.

WELLWYN. [*Delicately.*] Yes; yes—I remember, you found it difficult to stay long in any particular—yes.

FERRAND. [*Proudly.*] In one little corner? No—Monsieur—never! That is not in my character. I must see life.

WELLWYN. Quite, quite! Have some cake?
[*He cuts cake.*

FERRAND. In your country they say you cannot eat the cake and have it. But one must always try, Monsieur; one must never be content. [*Refusing the cake.*] *Grand merci*, but for the moment I have no stomach—I have lost my stomach now for two days. If I could smoke, Monsieur! [*He makes the gesture of smoking.*

WELLWYN. Rather! [*Handing his tobacco pouch.*] Roll yourself one.

FERRAND. [*Rapidly rolling a cigarette.*] If I had not found you, Monsieur—I would have been a little hole in the river to-night—I was so discouraged. [*He inhales and puffs a long luxurious whiff of smoke. Very bitterly.*]

Life! [*He disperses the puff of smoke with his finger, and stares before him.*] And to think that in a few minutes HE will be born! Monsieur! [*He gazes intently at* WELL-WYN.] The world would reproach you for your goodness to me.

WELLWYN. [*Looking uneasily at the door into the house.*] You think so? Ah!

FERRAND. Monsieur, if HE himself were on earth now, there would be a little heap of gentlemen writing to the journals every day to call Him sloppee sentimentalist! And what is veree funny, these gentlemen they would all be most strong Christians. [*He regards* WELLWYN *deeply.*] But that will not trouble you, Monsieur; I saw well from the first that you are no Christian. You have so kind a face.

WELLWYN. Oh! Indeed!

FERRAND. You have not enough the Pharisee in your character. You do not judge, and you are judged.

　　　　　　[*He stretches his limbs as if in pain.*

WELLWYN. Are you in pain?

FERRAND. I 'ave a little the rheumatism

WELLWYN. Wet through, of course! [*Glancing towards the house.*] Wait a bit! I wonder if you'd like these trousers; they've—er—they're not quite——

　　　[*He passes through the door into the house.* FER-
　　　　RAND *stands at the fire, with his limbs spread as
　　　　it were to embrace it, smoking with abandonment.*
　　　　WELLWYN *returns stealthily, dressed in a Jaeger
　　　　dressing-gown, and bearing a pair of drawers,
　　　　his trousers, a pair of slippers, and a sweater.*

WELLWYN. [*Speaking in a low voice, for the door is still open.*] Can you make these do for the moment?

FERRAND. *Je vous remercie, Monsieur.* [*Pointing to the screen.*] May I retire?

WELLWYN. Yes, yes.

> [FERRAND *goes behind the screen.* WELLWYN *closes the door into the house, then goes to the window to draw the curtains. He suddenly recoils and stands petrified with doubt.*

WELLWYN. Good Lord!

> [*There is the sound of tapping on glass. Against the window-pane is pressed the face of a man.* WELLWYN *motions to him to go away. He does not go, but continues tapping.* WELLWYN *opens the door. There enters a square old man, with a red, pendulous-jawed, shaking face under a snow besprinkled bowler hat. He is holding out a visiting card with tremulous hand.*

WELLWYN. Who's that? Who are you?

TIMSON. [*In a thick, hoarse, shaking voice.*] 'Appy to see you, sir; we 'ad a talk this morning. Timson—I give you me name. You invited of me, if ye remember.

WELLWYN. It's a little late, really.

TIMSON. Well, ye see, I never expected to 'ave to call on yer. I was 'itched up all right when I spoke to yer this mornin', but bein' Christmas, things 'ave took a turn with me to-day. [*He speaks with increasing thickness.*] I'm reg'lar disgusted—not got the price of a bed abaht me. Thought you wouldn't like me to be delicate—not at my age.

WELLWYN. [*With a mechanical and distracted dive of his hands into his pockets.*] The fact is, it so happens I haven't a copper on me.

TIMSON. [*Evidently taking this for professional refusal.*] Wouldn't arsk you if I could 'elp it. 'Ad to do with 'orses all me life. It's this 'ere cold I'm frightened of. I'm afraid I'll go to sleep.

WELLWYN. Well, really, I——

TIMSON. To be froze to death—I mean—it's awkward.

WELLWYN. [*Puzzled and unhappy.*] Well—come in a moment, and let's—think it out. Have some tea!

> [*He pours out the remains of the tea, and finding there is not very much, adds rum rather liberally. TIMSON, who walks a little wide at the knees, steadying his gait, has followed.*

TIMSON. [*Receiving the drink.*] Yer 'ealth. 'Ere's—soberiety! [*He applies the drink to his lips with shaking hand. Agreeably surprised.*] Blimey! Thish yer tea's foreign, ain't it?

FERRAND. [*Reappearing from behind the screen in his new clothes of which the trousers stop too soon.*] With a needle, Monsieur, I would soon have with what to make face against the world.

WELLWYN. Too short! Ah!

> [*He goes to the dais on which stands ANN's workbasket, and takes from it a needle and cotton.*
>
> [*While he is so engaged FERRAND is sizing up old TIMSON, as one dog will another. The old man, glass in hand, seems to have lapsed into coma.*

FERRAND. [*Indicating* TIMSON.] Monsieur!
> [*He makes the gesture of one drinking, and shakes his head.*

WELLWYN. [*Handing him the needle and cotton.*] Um! Afraid so!
> [*They approach* TIMSON, *who takes no notice.*

FERRAND. [*Gently.*] It is an old cabby, is it not, Monsieur? *Ceux sont tous des buveurs.*

WELLWYN. [*Concerned at the old man's stupefaction.*] Now, my old friend, sit down a moment. [*They manœuvre* TIMSON *to the settle.*] Will you smoke?

TIMSON. [*In a drowsy voice.*] Thank 'ee—smoke pipe of 'baccer. Old 'orse—standin' abaht in th' cold.
> [*He relapses into coma.*

FERRAND. [*With a click of his tongue.*] Il est parti.

WELLWYN. [*Doubtfully.*] He hasn't really left a horse outside, do you think?

FERRAND. *Non, non, Monsieur*—no 'orse. He is dreaming. I know very well that state of him—that catches you sometimes. It is the warmth sudden on the stomach. He will speak no more sense to-night. At the most, drink, and fly a little in his past.

WELLWYN. Poor old buffer!

FERRAND. Touching, is it not, Monsieur? There are many brave gents among the old cabbies—they have philosophy—that comes from 'orses, and from sitting still.

WELLWYN. [*Touching* TIMSON'S *shoulder.*] Drenched!

FERRAND. That will do 'im no 'arm, Monsieur—no 'arm at all. He is well wet inside, remember—it is

Christmas to-morrow. Put him a rug, if you will, he will soon steam.

> [WELLWYN *takes up* ANN's *long red cloak, and wraps it round the old man.*

TIMSON. [*Faintly roused.*] Tha's right. Put—the rug on th' old 'orse.

> [*He makes a strange noise, and works his head and tongue.*

WELLWYN. [*Alarmed.*] What's the matter with him?

FERRAND. It is nothing, Monsieur; for the moment he thinks 'imself a 'orse. *Il joue "cache-cache,"* 'ide and seek, with what you call—'is bitt.

WELLWYN. But what's to be done with him? One can't turn him out in this state.

FERRAND. If you wish to leave him 'ere, Monsieur, have no fear. I charge myself with him.

WELLWYN. Oh! [*Dubiously.*] You—er—I really don't know, I—hadn't contemplated—You think you could manage if I—if I went to bed?

FERRAND. But certainly, Monsieur.

WELLWYN. [*Still dubiously.*] You—you're sure you've everything you want?

FERRAND. [*Bowing.*] *Mais oui, Monsieur.*

WELLWYN. I don't know what I can do by staying.

FERRAND. There is nothing you can do, Monsieur. Have confidence in me.

WELLWYN. Well—keep the fire up quietly—very quietly. You'd better take this coat of mine, too. You'll find it precious cold, I expect, about three o'clock.   [*He hands* FERRAND *his ulster.*

FERRAND. [*Taking it.*] I shall sleep in praying for you, Monsieur.

WELLWYN. Ah! Yes! Thanks! Well—good-night! By the way, I shall be down rather early. Have to think of my household a bit, you know.

FERRAND. *Très bien, Monsieur.* I comprehend. One must well be regular in this life.

WELLWYN. [*With a start.*] Lord! [*He looks at the door of the model's room.*] I'd forgotten——

FERRAND. Can I undertake anything, Monsieur?

WELLWYN. No, no! [*He goes to the electric light switch by the outer door.*] You won't want this, will you?

FERRAND. *Merci, Monsieur.*

[WELLWYN *switches off the light.*

FERRAND. *Bon soir, Monsieur!*

WELLWYN. The devil! Er—good-night!

[*He hesitates, rumples his hair, and passes rather suddenly away.*

FERRAND. [*To himself.*] Poor pigeon! [*Looking long at old* TIMSON.] *Espèce de type anglais!*

[*He sits down in the firelight, curls up a foot on his knee, and taking out a knife, rips the stitching of a turned-up end of trouser, pinches the cloth double, and puts in the preliminary stitch of a new hem—all with the swiftness of one well-accustomed. Then, as if hearing a sound behind him, he gets up quickly and slips behind the screen.* MRS. MEGAN, *attracted by the cessation of voices, has opened the door, and is creeping from the model's room towards the fire. She has*

*almost reached it before she takes in the torpid
crimson figure of old* TIMSON. *She halts and
puts her hand to her chest—a queer figure in the
firelight, garbed in the canary-coloured bath
gown and rabbit's-wool slippers, her black matted
hair straggling down on her neck. Having quite
digested the fact that the old man is in a sort of
stupor,* MRS. MEGAN *goes close to the fire, and
sits on the little stool, smiling sideways at old*
TIMSON. FERRAND, *coming quietly up behind,
examines her from above, drooping his long nose
as if enquiring with it as to her condition in
life; then he steps back a yard or two.*

FERRAND. [*Gently.*] Pardon, Ma'moiselle.

MRS. MEGAN. [*Springing to her feet.*] Oh!

FERRAND. All right, all right! We are brave gents!

TIMSON. [*Faintly roused.*] 'Old up, there!

FERRAND. Trust in me, Ma'moiselle!

       [MRS. MEGAN *responds by drawing away.*

FERRAND. [*Gently.*] We must be good comrades.
This asylum—it is better than a doss-'ouse.

    [*He pushes the stool over towards her, and seats
       himself. Somewhat reassured,* MRS. MEGAN
       again sits down.

MRS. MEGAN. You frightened me.

TIMSON. [*Unexpectedly—in a drowsy tone.*] Purple
foreigners!

FERRAND. Pay no attention, Ma'moiselle. He is a
philosopher.

MRS. MEGAN. Oh! I thought 'e was boozed.

[*They both look at* TIMSON.

FERRAND. It is the same—veree 'armless.

MRS. MEGAN. What's that he's got on 'im?

FERRAND. It is a coronation robe. Have no fear, Ma'moiselle. Veree docile potentate.

MRS. MEGAN. I wouldn't be afraid of him. [*Challenging* FERRAND.] I'm afraid o' *you*.

FERRAND. It is because you do not know me, Ma'moiselle. You are wrong, it is always the unknown you should love.

MRS. MEGAN. I don't like the way you—speaks to me.

FERRAND. Ah! You are a Princess in disguise?

MRS. MEGAN. No fear!

FERRAND. No? What is it then you do to make face against the necessities of life? A living?

MRS. MEGAN. Sells flowers.

FERRAND. [*Rolling his eyes.*] It is not a career.

MRS. MEGAN. [*With a touch of devilry.*] You don't know what I do.

FERRAND. Ma'moiselle, whatever you do is charming.

[MRS. MEGAN *looks at him, and slowly smiles.*

MRS. MEGAN. You're a foreigner.

FERRAND. It is true.

MRS. MEGAN. What do *you* do for a livin'?

FERRAND. I am an interpreter.

MRS. MEGAN. You ain't very busy, are you?

FERRAND. [*With dignity.*] At present I am resting.

Mrs. Megan. [*Looking at him and smiling.*] How did you and 'im come here?

Ferrand. Ma'moiselle, we would ask you the same question.

Mrs. Megan. The gentleman let me. 'E's funny.

Ferrand. *C'est un ange!* [*At* Mrs. Megan's *blank stare he interprets.*] An angel!

Mrs. Megan. Me luck's out—that's why I come.

Ferrand. [*Rising.*] Ah! Ma'moiselle! Luck! There is the little God who dominates us all. Look at this old! [*He points to* Timson.] He is finished. In his day that old would be doing good business. He could afford himself— [*He makes a sign of drinking.*] Then come the motor cars. All goes—he has nothing left, only 'is 'abits of a cocher! Luck!

Timson. [*With a vague gesture—drowsily.*] Kick the foreign beggars out.

Ferrand. A real Englishman. . . . And look at me! My father was merchant of ostrich feathers in Brussels. If I had been content to go in his business, I would 'ave been rich. But I was born to roll—"rolling stone"— to voyage is stronger than myself. Luck! . . . And you, Ma'moiselle, shall I tell your fortune? [*He looks in her face.*] You were born for *la joie de vivre*—to drink the wines of life. *Et vous voilà!* Luck!

> [*Though she does not in the least understand what he has said, her expression changes to a sort of glee.*

Ferrand. Yes. You were born loving pleasure. Is it not? You see, you cannot say, No. All of us, we have our fates. Give me your hand. [*He kneels down and takes her hand.*] In each of us there is that against which we cannot struggle. Yes, yes!

> [*He holds her hand, and turns it over between his own.* MRS. MEGAN *remains stolid, half-fasci-nated, half-reluctant.*

TIMSON. [*Flickering into consciousness.*] Be'ave your-selves! Yer crimson canary birds!

> [MRS. MEGAN *would withdraw her hand, but cannot.*

FERRAND. Pay no attention, Ma'moiselle. He is a Puritan.

> [TIMSON *relapses into comatosity, upsetting his glass, which falls with a crash.*

MRS. MEGAN. Let go my hand, please!

FERRAND. [*Relinquishing it, and staring into the fire gravely.*] There is one thing I have never done—'urt a woman—that is hardly in my character. [*Then, draw-ing a little closer, he looks into her face.*] Tell me, Ma'-moiselle, what is it you think of all day long?

MRS. MEGAN. I dunno—lots, I thinks of.

FERRAND. Shall I tell you? [*Her eyes remain fixed on his, the strangeness of him preventing her from telling him to "get along." He goes on in his ironic voice.*] It is of the streets—the lights—the faces—it is of all which moves, and is warm—it is of colour—it is [*he brings his face quite close to hers*] of Love. That is for you what the road is for me. That is for you what the rum is for that old— [*He jerks his thumb back at* TIMSON. *Then bending swiftly forward to the girl.*] See! I kiss you—Ah!

> [*He draws her forward off the stool. There is a little struggle, then she resigns her lips. The*

little stool, overturned, falls with a clatter. They spring up, and move apart. The door opens and ANN *enters from the house in a blue dressing-gown, with her hair loose, and a candle held high above her head. Taking in the strange half-circle round the stove, she recoils. Then, standing her ground, calls in a voice sharpened by fright:* "Daddy—Daddy!"

TIMSON. [*Stirring uneasily, and struggling to his feet.*] All ri——! I'm comin'!

FERRAND. Have no fear, Madame!

[*In the silence that follows, a clock begins loudly striking twelve.* ANN *remains, as if carved in stone, her eyes fastened on the strangers. There is the sound of someone falling downstairs, and* WELLWYN *appears, also holding a candle above his head.*

ANN. Look!

WELLWYN. Yes, yes, my dear! It—it happened.

ANN. [*With a sort of groan.*] Oh! Daddy!

[*In the renewed silence, the church clock ceases to chime.*

FERRAND. [*Softly, in his ironic voice.*] HE is come, Monsieur! 'Appy Christmas! Bon Noël!

[*There is a sudden chime of bells. The Stage is blotted dark.*

Curtain.

ACT II

It is four o'clock in the afternoon of New Year's Day. On the raised dais MRS. MEGAN *is standing, in her rags; with bare feet and ankles, her dark hair as if blown about, her lips parted, holding out a dishevelled bunch of violets. Before his easel,* WELLWYN *is painting her. Behind him, at a table between the cupboard and the door to the model's room,* TIMSON *is washing brushes, with the movements of one employed upon relief works. The samovar is hissing on the table by the stove, the tea things are set out.*

WELLWYN. Open your mouth.

        [MRS. MEGAN *opens her mouth.*
ANN. [*In hat and coat, entering from the house.*] Daddy!

      [WELLWYN *goes to her; and, released from restraint,* MRS. MEGAN *looks round at* TIMSON *and grimaces.*
WELLWYN. Well, my dear?

        [*They speak in low voices.*
ANN. [*Holding out a note.*] This note from Canon Bertley. He's going to bring her husband here this afternoon.   [*She looks at* MRS. MEGAN.
WELLWYN. Oh!   [*He also looks at* MRS. MEGAN.

27

Ann. And I met Sir Thomas Hoxton at church this morning, and spoke to him about Timson.

Wellwyn. Um!

> [*They look at* Timson. *Then* Ann *goes back to the door, and* Wellwyn *follows her.*

Ann. [*Turning.*] I'm going round now, Daddy, to ask Professor Calway what we're to do with that Ferrand.

Wellwyn. Oh! One each! I wonder if they'll like it.

Ann. They'll have to lump it.

> [*She goes out into the house.*

Wellwyn. [*Back at his easel.*] You can shut your mouth now.

> [Mrs. Megan *shuts her mouth, but opens it immediately to smile.*

Wellwyn. [*Spasmodically.*] Ah! Now that's what I want. [*He dabs furiously at the canvas. Then standing back, runs his hands through his hair and turns a painter's glance towards the skylight.*] Dash! Light's gone! Off you get, child—don't tempt me!

> [Mrs. Megan *descends. Passing towards the door of the model's room she stops, and stealthily looks at the picture.*

Timson. Ah! Would yer!

Wellwyn. [*Wheeling round.*] Want to have a look? Well—come on!

> [*He takes her by the arm, and they stand before the canvas. After a stolid moment, she giggles.*

Wellwyn. Oh! You think so?

MRS. MEGAN. [*Who has lost her hoarseness.*] It's not like my picture that I had on the pier.

WELLWYN. No—it wouldn't be.

MRS. MEGAN. [*Timidly.*] If I had an 'at on, I'd look better.

WELLWYN. With feathers?

MRS. MEGAN. Yes.

WELLWYN. Well, you can't! I don't like hats, and I don't like feathers.

> [MRS. MEGAN *timidly tugs his sleeve.* TIMSON, *screened as he thinks by the picture, has drawn from his bulky pocket a bottle and is taking a stealthy swig.*

WELLWYN. [*To* MRS. MEGAN, *affecting not to notice.*] How much do I owe you?

MRS. MEGAN. [*A little surprised.*] You paid me for to-day—all 'cept a penny.

WELLWYN. Well! Here it is. [*He gives her a coin.*] Go and get your feet on!

MRS. MEGAN. You've give me 'arf a crown.

WELLWYN. Cut away now!

> [MRS. MEGAN, *smiling at the coin, goes towards the model's room. She looks back at* WELLWYN, *as if to draw his eyes to her, but he is gazing at the picture; then, catching old* TIMSON'S *sour glance, she grimaces at him, kicking up her feet with a little squeal. But when* WELLWYN *turns to the sound, she is demurely passing through the doorway.*

TIMSON. [*In his voice of dubious sobriety.*] I've finished these yer brushes, sir. It's not a man's work.
I've been thinkin' if you'd keep an 'orse, I could give
yer satisfaction.

WELLWYN. Would the horse, Timson?

TIMSON. [*Looking him up and down.*] I knows of one
that would just suit yer. Reel 'orse, you'd like 'im.

WELLWYN. [*Shaking his head.*] Afraid not, Timson!
Awfully sorry, though, to have nothing better for you
than this, at present.

TIMSON. [*Faintly waving the brushes.*] Of course, if
you can't afford it, I don't press you—it's only that I
feel I'm not doing meself justice. [*Confidentially.*]
There's just one thing, sir; I can't bear to see a gen'leman imposed on. That foreigner—'e's not the sort to
'ave about the place. Talk? Oh! ah! But 'e'll never
do any good with 'imself. He's a alien.

WELLWYN. Terrible misfortune to a fellow, Timson.

TIMSON. Don't you believe it, sir; it's his *fault* I
says to the young lady yesterday: Miss Ann, your
father's a gen'leman [*with a sudden accent of hoarse sincerity*], and so you are—I don't mind sayin' it—*but*, I
said, he's too easy-goin'.

WELLWYN. Indeed!

TIMSON. Well, see that girl now! [*He shakes his head.*]
I never did believe in goin' behind a person's back—
I'm an Englishman—but [*lowering his voice*] she's a
bad hat, sir. Why, look at the street she comes from!

WELLWYN. Oh! you know it.

TIMSON. Lived there meself larst three years. See

the difference a few days' corn's made in her.   She's
that saucy you can't touch 'er head.

WELLWYN. Is there any necessity, Timson?

TIMSON. Artful too.   Full o' vice, I call 'er.   Where's
'er 'usband?

WELLWYN. [*Gravely.*] Come, Timson!   You wouldn't
like *her* to——

TIMSON. [*With dignity, so that the bottle in his pocket
is plainly visible.*] I'm a man as always beared inspec-
tion.

WELLWYN. [*With a well-directed smile.*] So I see.

TIMSON. [*Curving himself round the bottle.*] It's not
for me to say nothing—but I can tell a gen'leman as
quick as ever I can tell an 'orse.

WELLWYN. [*Painting.*] I find it safest to assume
that every man is a gentleman, and every woman a
lady.   Saves no end of self-contempt.   Give me the
little brush.

TIMSON. [*Handing him the brush—after a consider-
able introspective pause.*] Would yer like me to stay and
wash it for yer again?   [*With great resolution.*] I will—
I'll do it for you—never grudged workin' for a gen'leman.

WELLWYN. [*With sincerity.*] Thank you, Timson—
very good of you, I'm sure.   [*He hands him back the
brush.*] Just lend us a hand with this.   [*Assisted by* TIM-
SON *he pushes back the dais.*] Let's see!   What do I owe
you?

TIMSON. [*Reluctantly.*] It so 'appens, you advanced
me to-day's yesterday.

WELLWYN. Then I suppose you want to-morrow's?

TIMSON. Well, I 'ad to spend it, lookin' for a permanent job. When you've got to do with 'orses, you can't neglect the publics, or you might as well be dead.

WELLWYN. Quite so!

TIMSON. It mounts up in the course o' the year.

WELLWYN. It would. [*Passing him a coin.*] This is for an exceptional purpose—Timson—see. Not——

TIMSON. [*Touching his forehead.*] Certainly, sir. I quite understand. I'm not that sort, as I think I've proved to yer, comin' here regular day after day, all the week. There's one thing, I ought to warn you perhaps—I might 'ave to give this job up any day.

> [*He makes a faint demonstration with the little brush, then puts it, absent-mindedly, into his pocket.*

WELLWYN. [*Gravely.*] I'd never stand in the way of your bettering yourself, Timson. And, by the way, my daughter spoke to a friend about you to-day. I think something may come of it.

TIMSON. Oh! Oh! She did! Well, it might do me a bit o' good. [*He makes for the outer door, but stops.*] That foreigner! 'E sticks in my gizzard. It's not as if there wasn't plenty o' pigeons for 'im to pluck in 'is own Gawd-forsaken country. Reg-lar jay, that's what I calls 'im. I could tell yer something——

> [*He has opened the door, and suddenly sees that FERRAND himself is standing there. Sticking out his lower lip, TIMSON gives a roll of his jaw*

*and lurches forth into the street. Owing to a
slight miscalculation, his face and raised arms
are plainly visible through the window, as he for-
tifies himself from his battle against the cold.*
FERRAND, *having closed the door, stands with
his thumb acting as pointer towards this spectacle.
He is now remarkably dressed in an artist's
squashy green hat, a frock coat too small for him,
a bright blue tie of knitted silk, the grey trousers
that were torn, well-worn brown boots, and a tan
waistcoat.*

WELLWYN. What luck to-day?

FERRAND. [*With a shrug.*] Again I have beaten all
London, Monsieur—not one bite. [*Contemplating himself.*] I think perhaps, that, for the bourgeoisie, there is
a little too much colour in my costume.

WELLWYN. [*Contemplating him.*] Let's see—I believe I've an old top hat somewhere.

FERRAND. Ah! Monsieur, *merci,* but *that* I could
not. It is scarcely in my character.

WELLWYN. True!

FERRAND. I have been to merchants of wine, of *tabac,*
to hotels, to Leicester Square. I have been to a—
Society for spreading Christian knowledge—I thought
there I would have a chance perhaps as interpreter.
Toujours même chose—we regret, we have no situation
for you—same thing everywhere. It seems there is
nothing doing in this town.

WELLWYN. I've noticed, there never is.

FERRAND. I was thinking, Monsieur, that in **avia-**

tion there might be a career for me—but it seems one must be trained.

WELLWYN. Afraid so, Ferrand.

FERRAND. [*Approaching the picture.*] Ah! You are always working at this. You will have something of very good there, Monsieur. You wish to fix the type of wild savage existing ever amongst our high civilisation. *C'est très chic ça!* [WELLWYN *manifests the quiet delight of an English artist actually understood.*] In the figures of these good citizens, to whom she offers her flower, you would give the idea of all the cage doors open to catch and make tame the wild bird, that will surely die within. *Très gentil!* Believe me, Monsieur, you have there the greatest comedy of life! How anxious are the tame birds to do the wild birds good. [*His voice changes.*] For the wild birds it is not funny. There is in some human souls, Monsieur, what cannot be made tame.

WELLWYN. I believe you, Ferrand.

> [*The face of a young man appears at the window, unseen. Suddenly* ANN *opens the door leading to the house.*

ANN. Daddy—I want you.

WELLWYN. [*To* FERRAND.] Excuse me a minute!

> [*He goes to his daughter, and they pass out.*
> [FERRAND *remains at the picture.* MRS. MEGAN *dressed in some of* ANN'S *discarded garments, has come out of the model's room. She steals up behind* FERRAND *like a cat, reaches an arm up, and curls it round his mouth. He turns, and*

tries to seize her; she disingenuously slips away.
He follows. The chase circles the tea table. He
catches her, lifts her up, swings round with her,
so that her feet fly out; kisses her bent-back face,
and sets her down. She stands there smiling.
The face at the window darkens.

FERRAND. La Valse!

[*He takes her with both hands by the waist, she puts*
her hands against his shoulders to push him off
—and suddenly they are whirling. As they
whirl, they bob together once or twice, and kiss.
Then, with a warning motion towards the door,
she wrenches herself free, and stops beside the
picture, trying desperately to appear demure.
WELLWYN *and* ANN *have entered. The face*
has vanished.

FERRAND. [*Pointing to the picture.*] One does not
comprehend all this, Monsieur, without well studying.
I was in train to interpret for Ma'moiselle the chiaro-
scuro.

WELLWYN. [*With a queer look.*] Don't take it *too*
seriously, Ferrand.

FERRAND. It is a masterpiece.

WELLWYN. My daughter's just spoken to a friend,
Professor Calway. He'd like to meet you. Could you
come back a little later?

FERRAND. Certainly, Ma'moiselle. That will be an
opening for me, I trust. [*He goes to the street door.*

ANN. [*Paying no attention to him.*] Mrs. Megan, will
you too come back in half an hour?

FERRAND. *Très bien, Ma'moiselle!* I will see that she does. We will take a little promenade together. That will do us good.

> [*He motions towards the door;* MRS. MEGAN, *all eyes, follows him out.*]

ANN. Oh! Daddy, they *are* rotters. Couldn't you *see* they were having the most high jinks?

WELLWYN. [*At his picture.*] I seemed to have noticed something.

ANN. [*Preparing for tea.*] They were kissing.

WELLWYN. Tt! Tt!

ANN. They're hopeless, all three—especially her. Wish I hadn't given her my clothes now.

WELLWYN. [*Absorbed.*] Something of wild-savage.

ANN. Thank goodness it's the Vicar's business to see that married people live together in his parish.

WELLWYN. Oh! [*Dubiously.*] The Megans are Roman Catholic-Atheists, Ann.

ANN. [*With heat.*] Then they're all the more bound.

> [WELLWYN *gives a sudden and alarmed whistle.*]

ANN. What's the matter?

WELLWYN. Didn't you say you spoke to Sir Thomas, too. Suppose he comes in while the Professor's here. They're cat and dog.

ANN. [*Blankly.*] Oh! [*As* WELLWYN *strikes a match.*] The samovar *is* lighted. [*Taking up the nearly empty decanter of rum and going to the cupboard.*] It's all right. He won't.

WELLWYN. We'll hope not.

> [*He turns back to his picture.*]

ANN. [*At the cupboard.*] Daddy!

WELLWYN. Hi!

ANN. There were *three bottles*.

WELLWYN. Oh!

ANN. Well! Now there aren't any.

WELLWYN. [*Abstracted.*] That'll be Timson.

ANN. [*With real horror.*] But it's awful!

WELLWYN. It is, my dear.

ANN. In seven days. To say nothing of the stealing.

WELLWYN. [*Vexed.*] I blame myself—very much. Ought to have kept it locked up.

ANN. You ought to keep *him* locked up!

> [*There is heard a mild but authoritative knock.*

WELLWYN. Here's the Vicar!

ANN. What are you going to do about the rum?

WELLWYN. [*Opening the door to* CANON BERTLEY.] Come in, Vicar! Happy New Year!

BERTLEY. Same to you! Ah! Ann! I've got into touch with her young husband—he's coming round.

ANN. [*Still a little out of her plate.*] Thank Go—— Moses!

BERTLEY. [*Faintly surprised.*] From what I hear he's not really a bad youth. Afraid he bets on horses. The great thing, Wellwyn, with those poor fellows is to put your finger on the weak spot.

ANN. [*To herself—gloomily.*] *That's* not difficult. What would you do, Canon Bertley, with a man who's been drinking father's rum?

BERTLEY. Remove the temptation, of course.

WELLWYN. He's done that.

BERTLEY. Ah! Then— [WELLWYN *and* ANN *hang on his words*] then I should—er——

ANN. [*Abruptly.*] Remove *him*.

BERTLEY. Before I say that, Ann, I must certainly see the individual.

WELLWYN. [*Pointing to the window.*] There he is!
　　　[*In the failing light* TIMSON'S *face is indeed to be seen pressed against the window pane.*

ANN. Daddy, I do wish you'd have thick glass put in. It's so disgusting to be spied at! [WELLWYN *going quickly to the door, has opened it.*] What do you want?
　　　　　　[TIMSON *enters with dignity. He is fuddled.*

TIMSON. [*Slowly.*] Arskin' yer pardon—thought it me duty to come back—found thish yer little brishel on me. 　　　　[*He produces the little paint brush.*

ANN. [*In a deadly voice.*] Nothing else?
　　　　　　　　[TIMSON *accords her a glassy stare.*

WELLWYN. [*Taking the brush hastily.*] That'll do, Timson, thanks!

TIMSON. As I am 'ere, can I do anything for yer?

ANN. Yes, you can sweep out that little room. [*She points to the model's room.*] There's a broom in there.

TIMSON. [*Disagreeably surprised.*] Certainly; never make bones about a little extra—never 'ave in all me life. Do it at onsh, I will. [*He moves across to the model's room at that peculiar broad gait so perfectly adjusted to his habits.*] You quite understand me—couldn't bear to 'ave anything on me that wasn't mine.
　　　　　　　　　　　　　　[*He passes out.*

ANN. Old fraud!

WELLWYN. "In" and "on." Mark my words, he'll restore the—bottles.

BERTLEY. But, my dear Wellwyn, that *is* stealing.

WELLWYN. We all have our discrepancies, Vicar.

ANN. Daddy! Discrepancies!

WELLWYN. Well, Ann, my theory is that as regards solids Timson's an Individualist, but as regards liquids he's a Socialist . . . or *vice versâ*, according to taste.

BERTLEY. No, no, we mustn't joke about it. [*Gravely.*] I do think he should be spoken to.

WELLWYN. Yes, but not by me.

BERTLEY. Surely you're the proper person.

WELLWYN. [*Shaking his head.*] It was my rum, Vicar. Look so personal.

> [*There sound a number of little tat-tat knocks.*

WELLWYN. Isn't that the Professor's knock?

> [*While Ann sits down to make tea, he goes to the door and opens it. There, dressed in an ulster, stands a thin, clean-shaved man, with a little hollow sucked into either cheek, who, taking off a grey squash hat, discloses a majestically bald forehead, which completely dominates all that comes below it.*

WELLWYN. Come in, Professor! So awfully good of you! You know Canon Bertley, I think?

CALWAY. Ah! How d'you do?

WELLWYN. Your opinion will be invaluable, Professor.

ANN. Tea, Professor Calway?

> [*They have assembled round the tea table.*

CALWAY. Thank you; no tea; milk.

WELLWYN. Rum?

> [*He pours rum into* CALWAY's *milk.*

CALWAY. A little—thanks! [*Turning to* ANN.] You were going to show me some one you're trying to rescue, or something, I think.

ANN. Oh! Yes. He'll be here directly—simply perfect rotter.

CALWAY. [*Smiling.*] Really! Ah! I think you said he was a congenital?

WELLWYN. [*With great interest.*] What!

ANN. [*Low.*] Daddy! [*To* CALWAY.] Yes; I—I think that's what you call him.

CALWAY. Not old?

ANN. No; and quite healthy—a vagabond.

CALWAY. [*Sipping.*] I see! Yes. Is it, do you think chronic unemployment with a vagrant tendency? Or would it be nearer the mark to say: Vagrancy——

WELLWYN. Pure! Oh! pure! Professor. Awfully human.

CALWAY. [*With a smile of knowledge.*] Quite! And —er——

ANN. [*Breaking in.*] Before he comes, there's another——

BERTLEY. [*Blandly.*] Yes, when you came in, we were discussing what should be done with a man who drinks rum— [CALWAY *pauses in the act of drinking*] that doesn't belong to him.

CALWAY. Really! Dipsomaniac?

BERTLEY. Well—perhaps you could tell us—drink

certainly changing thine to mine.   The Professor could
see him, Wellwyn?

ANN. [*Rising.*] Yes, do come and look at him, Professor Calway.   He's in there.

> [*She points towards the model's room.* CALWAY
> *smiles deprecatingly.*

ANN. No, *really;* we needn't open the door.   You
can see him through the glass.   He's more than half——

CALWAY. Well, I hardly——

ANN. Oh!   Do!   Come on, Professor Calway!   We
must know what to do with him. [CALWAY *rises.*]
You can stand on a chair.   It's all science.

> [*She draws* CALWAY *to the model's room, which is
> lighted by a glass panel in the top of the high door.*
> CANON BERTLEY *also rises and stands watch-
> ing.* WELLWYN *hovers, torn between respect for
> science and dislike of espionage.*

ANN. [*Drawing up a chair.*] Come on!

CALWAY. Do you seriously wish me to?

ANN. Rather!   It's quite safe; he can't see you.

CALWAY. But he might come out.

> [ANN *puts her back against the door.* CALWAY
> *mounts the chair dubiously, and raises his head
> cautiously, bending it more and more downwards.*

ANN. Well?

CALWAY. He appears to be—sitting on the floor.

WELLWYN. Yes, that's all right!

>   [BERTLEY *covers his lips.*

CALWAY. [*To* ANN—*descending.*] By the look of his

face, as far as one can see it, I should say there was a leaning towards mania. I know the treatment.

> [*There come three loud knocks on the door.* WELL-
> WYN *and* ANN *exchange a glance of consterna-
> tion.*

ANN. Who's that?

WELLWYN. It sounds like Sir Thomas.

CALWAY. Sir Thomas Hoxton?

WELLWYN. [*Nodding.*] Awfully sorry, Professor. You see, we——

CALWAY. Not at all. Only, I must decline to be involved in argument with him, please.

BERTLEY. He has experience. We might get his opinion, don't you think?

CALWAY. On a point of reform? A J.P.!

BERTLEY. [*Deprecating.*] My dear Sir—we needn't take it.

> [*The three knocks resound with extraordinary fury.*

ANN. You'd better open the door, Daddy.

> [WELLWYN *opens the door.* SIR THOMAS HOX-
> TON *is disclosed in a fur overcoat and top hat.
> His square, well-coloured face is remarkable for
> a massive jaw, dominating all that comes above
> it. His voice is resolute.*

HOXTON. Afraid I didn't make myself heard.

WELLWYN. So good of you to come, Sir Thomas. Canon Bertley! [*They greet.*] Professor Calway you know, I think.

HOXTON. [*Ominously.*] I do.

> [*They almost greet. An awkward pause.*

ANN. [*Blurting it out.*] That old cabman I told you of's been drinking father's rum.

BERTLEY. We were just discussing what's to be done with him, Sir Thomas. One wants to do the very best, of course. The question of reform is always delicate.

CALWAY. I beg your pardon. There *is* no question here.

HOXTON. [*Abruptly.*] Oh! Is he in the house?

ANN. In there.

HOXTON. Works for you, eh?

WELLWYN. Er—yes.

HOXTON. Let's have a look at him!

                     [*An embarrassed pause.*

BERTLEY. Well—the fact is, Sir Thomas——

CALWAY. When last under observation——

ANN. He was sitting on the floor.

WELLWYN. I don't want the old fellow to feel he's being made a show of. Disgusting to be spied at, Ann.

ANN. You can't, Daddy! He's drunk.

HOXTON. Never mind, Miss Wellwyn. Hundreds of these fellows before me in my time. [*At* CALWAY.] The only thing is a sharp lesson!

CALWAY. I disagree. I've seen the man; what he requires is steady control, and the Dobbins treatment.

    [WELLWYN *approaches them with fearful interest.*

HOXTON. Not a bit of it! He wants one for his knob! Brace 'em up! It's the only thing.

BERTLEY. Personally, I think that if he were spoken to seriously——

CALWAY. I cannot walk arm in arm with a crab!

HOXTON. [*Approaching* CALWAY.] I beg your pardon?

CALWAY. [*Moving back a little.*] You're moving backwards, Sir Thomas. I've told you before, convinced reactionaryism, in these days——

[*There comes a single knock on the street door.*

BERTLEY. [*Looking at his watch.*] D'you know, I'm rather afraid this may be our young husband, Wellwyn. I told him half-past four.

WELLWYN. Oh! Ah! Yes. [*Going towards the two reformers.*] Shall we go into the house, Professor, and settle the question quietly while the Vicar sees a young man?

CALWAY. [*Pale with uncompleted statement, and gravitating insensibly in the direction indicated.*] The merest sense of continuity—a simple instinct for order——

HOXTON. [*Following.*] The only way to get order, sir, is to bring the disorderly up with a round turn. [CALWAY *turns to him in the doorway.*] You people without practical experience——

CALWAY. If you'll listen to me a minute.

HOXTON. I can show you in a mo——

[*They vanish through the door.*

WELLWYN. I was afraid of it.

BERTLEY. The two points of view. Pleasant to see such keenness. I may want you, Wellwyn. And Ann perhaps had better not be present.

WELLWYN. [*Relieved.*] Quite so! My dear!

[ANN *goes reluctantly.* WELLWYN *opens the street door. The lamp outside has just been lighted, and, by its gleam, is seen the figure of*

RORY MEGAN, *thin, pale, youthful.* ANN *turning at the door into the house gives him a long, inquisitive look, then goes.*

WELLWYN. Is that Megan?

MEGAN. Yus.

WELLWYN. Come in.

[MEGAN *comes in. There follows an awkward silence, during which* WELLWYN *turns up the light, then goes to the tea table and pours out a glass of tea and rum.*

BERTLEY. [*Kindly.*] Now, my boy, how is it that you and your wife are living apart like this?

MEGAN. I dunno.

BERTLEY. Well, if *you* don't, none of us are very likely to, are we?

MEGAN. That's what I thought, as I was comin' along.

WELLWYN. [*Twinkling.*] Have some tea, Megan? [*Handing him the glass.*] What d'you think of her picture? 'Tisn't quite finished.

MEGAN. [*After scrutiny.*] I seen her look like it— once.

WELLWYN. Good! When was that?

MEGAN. [*Stoically.*] When she 'ad the measles.

[*He drinks.*

WELLWYN. [*Ruminating.*] I see—yes. I quite see— feverish!

BERTLEY. My dear Wellwyn, let me—— [*To* ME-GAN.] Now, I hope you're willing to come together again, and to maintain her?

MEGAN. If she'll maintain me.

BERTLEY. Oh! but—— I see, you mean you're in the same line of business?

MEGAN. Yus.

BERTLEY. And lean on each other. Quite so!

MEGAN. I leans on 'er mostly—with 'er looks.

BERTLEY. Indeed! Very interesting—that!

MEGAN. Yus. Sometimes she'll take 'arf a crown off of a toff.   [*He looks at* WELLWYN.

WELLWYN. [*Twinkling.*] I apologise to you, Megan.

MEGAN. [*With a faint smile.*] I could do with a bit more of it.

BERTLEY. [*Dubiously.*] Yes! Yes! Now, my boy, I've heard you bet on horses.

MEGAN. No, I don't.

BERTLEY. Play cards, then? Come! Don't be afraid to acknowledge it.

MEGAN. When I'm 'ard up—yus.

BERTLEY. But don't you know that's ruination?

MEGAN. Depends. Sometimes I wins a lot.

BERTLEY. You know that's not at all what I mean. Come, promise me to give it up.

MEGAN. I dunno abaht that.

BERTLEY. Now, there's a good fellow. Make a big effort and throw the habit off!

MEGAN. Comes over me—same as it might over you.

BERTLEY. Over me! How do you mean, my boy?

MEGAN. [*With a look up.*] To tork!

    [WELLWYN, *turning to the picture, makes a funny little noise.*

BERTLEY. [*Maintaining his good humour.*] A hit! But you forget, you know, to talk's my business. It's not yours to gamble.

MEGAN. You try sellin' flowers. If that ain't a— gamble——

BERTLEY. I'm afraid we're wandering a little from the point. Husband and wife should be together. You were brought up to that. Your father and mother——

MEGAN. Never was.

WELLWYN. [*Turning from the picture.*] The question is, Megan: Will you take your wife home? She's a good little soul.

MEGAN. She never let me know it.

[*There is a feeble knock on the door.*

WELLWYN. Well, now come. Here she is!

[*He points to the door, and stands regarding*
MEGAN *with his friendly smile.*

MEGAN. [*With a gleam of responsiveness.*] I might, perhaps, to please *you*, sir.

BERTLEY. [*Appropriating the gesture.*] Capital, I thought we should get on in time.

MEGAN. Yus.

[WELLWYN *opens the door.* MRS. MEGAN *and*
FERRAND *are revealed. They are about to enter,
but catching sight of* MEGAN, *hesitate.*

BERTLEY. Come in! Come in!

[MRS. MEGAN *enters stolidly.* FERRAND, *following, stands apart with an air of extreme detach-
ment.* MEGAN, *after a quick glance at them*

*both, remains unmoved. No one has noticed
that the door of the model's room has been opened,
and that the unsteady figure of old* TIMSON *is
standing there.*

BERTLEY. [*A little awkward in the presence of* FER-
RAND—*to the* MEGANS.] This begins a new chapter.
We won't improve the occasion. No need.

[MEGAN, *turning towards his wife, makes her a
gesture as if to say:* "Here! let's get out of
this!"

BERTLEY. Yes, yes, you'll like to get home at once
—I know.   [*He holds up his hand mechanically.*

TIMSON. I forbids the banns.

BERTLEY. [*Startled.*] Gracious!

TIMSON. [*Extremely unsteady.*] Just cause and im-
pejiment. There 'e stands. [*He points to* FERRAND.]
The crimson foreigner! The mockin' jay!

WELLWYN. Timson!

TIMSON. You're a gen'leman—I'm aweer o' that—
but I must speak the truth—[*he waves his hand*] an'
shame the devil!

BERTLEY. Is this the rum——?

TIMSON. [*Struck by the word.*] I'm a teetotaler.

WELLWYN. Timson, Timson!

TIMSON. Seein' as there's ladies present, I won't be
conspicuous. [*Moving away, and making for the door,
he strikes against the dais, and mounts upon it.*] But what
I do say, is: He's no better than 'er and she's worse.

BERTLEY. This is distressing.

FERRAND. [*Calmly.*] On my honour, Monsieur!

[TIMSON *growls.*

WELLWYN. Now, now, Timson!

TIMSON. That's all right. You're a gen'leman, an' I'm a gen'leman, but he ain't an' she ain't.

WELLWYN. We shall not believe you.

BERTLEY. No, no; we shall not believe you.

TIMSON. [*Heavily.*] Very well, you doubts my word. Will it make any difference, Guv'nor, if I speaks the truth?

BERTLEY. No, certainly not—that is—of course, it will.

TIMSON. Well, then, I see 'em plainer than I see [*pointing at* BERTLEY] the two of you.

WELLWYN. Be quiet, Timson!

BERTLEY. Not even her husband believes you.

MEGAN. [*Suddenly.*] Don't I!

WELLWYN. Come, Megan, you can see the old fellow's in Paradise.

BERTLEY. Do you credit such a—such an object?

[*He points at* TIMSON, *who seems falling asleep.*

MEGAN. Naow!

[*Unseen by anybody,* ANN *has returned.*

BERTLEY. Well, then, my boy?

MEGAN. I seen 'em meself.

BERTLEY. Gracious! But just now you were willing——

MEGAN. [*Sardonically.*] There wasn't nothing against me honour, then. Now you've took it away between you, comin' aht with it like this. I don't want no more of 'er, and I'll want a good deal more of 'im; as 'e'll soon find.

[*He jerks his chin at* FERRAND, *turns slowly on his heel, and goes out into the street.*

[*There follows a profound silence.*

ANN. What did I say, Daddy? Utter! All three.

[*Suddenly alive to her presence, they all turn.*

TIMSON. [*Waking up and looking round him.*] Well, p'raps I'd better go.

[*Assisted by* WELLWYN *he lurches gingerly off the dais towards the door, which* WELLWYN *holds open for him.*

TIMSON. [*Mechanically.*] Where to, sir?

[*Receiving no answer he passes out, touching his hat; and the door is closed.*

WELLWYN. Ann!

[ANN *goes back whence she came.*

[BERTLEY, *steadily regarding* MRS. MEGAN, *who has put her arm up in front of her face, beckons to* FERRAND, *and the young man comes gravely forward.*

BERTLEY. Young people, this is very dreadful. [MRS. MEGAN *lowers her arm a little, and looks at him over it.*] Very sad!

MRS. MEGAN. [*Dropping her arm.*] Megan's no better than what I am.

BERTLEY. Come, come! Here's your home broken up! [MRS. MEGAN *smiles. Shaking his head gravely.*] Surely—surely—you mustn't smile. [MRS. MEGAN *becomes tragic.*] That's better. Now, what is to be done?

FERRAND. Believe me, Monsieur, I greatly regret.

BERTLEY. I'm glad to hear it.

FERRAND. If I had foreseen this disaster.

BERTLEY. Is that your only reason for regret?

FERRAND. [*With a little bow.*] Any reason that you wish, Monsieur. I will do my possible.

MRS. MEGAN. I could get an unfurnished room if [*she slides her eyes round at* WELLWYN] I 'ad the money to furnish it.

BERTLEY. But suppose I can induce your husband to forgive you, and take you back?

MRS. MEGAN. [*Shaking her head.*] 'E'd 'it me.

BERTLEY. I said to forgive.

MRS. MEGAN. That wouldn't make no difference. [*With a flash at* BERTLEY.] An' I ain't forgiven him!

BERTLEY. That is sinful.

MRS. MEGAN. *I'm* a Catholic.

BERTLEY. My good child, what difference does that make?

FERRAND. Monsieur, if I might interpret for her.

[BERTLEY *silences him with a gesture.*

MRS. MEGAN. [*Sliding her eyes towards* WELLWYN.] If I 'ad the money to buy some fresh stock.

BERTLEY. Yes; yes; never mind the money. What I want to find in you both, is repentance.

MRS. MEGAN. [*With a flash up at him.*] I can't get me livin' off of repentin'.

BERTLEY. Now, now! Never say what you know to be wrong.

FERRAND. Monsieur, her soul is very simple.

BERTLEY. [*Severely.*] I do not know, sir, that we shall get any great assistance from your views. In fact, one thing is clear to me, she must discontinue your acquaintanceship at once.

FERRAND. Certainly, Monsieur. We have no serious intentions.

BERTLEY. All the more shame to you, then!

FERRAND. Monsieur, I see perfectly your point of view. It is very natural. [*He bows and is silent.*

MRS. MEGAN. I don't want '*im* hurt 'cos o' me. Megan'll get his mates to belt him—bein' foreign like he is.

BERTLEY. Yes, never mind that. It's *you* I'm thinking of.

MRS. MEGAN. I'd sooner they'd hit *me*.

WELLWYN. [*Suddenly.*] Well said, my child!

MRS. MEGAN. 'Twasn't his fault.

FERRAND. [*Without irony—to* WELLWYN.] I cannot accept that Monsieur. The blame—it is all mine.

ANN. [*Entering suddenly from the house.*] Daddy, they're having an awful——!

> [*The voices of* PROFESSOR CALWAY *and* SIR
> THOMAS HOXTON *are distinctly heard.*

CALWAY. The question is a much wider one, Sir Thomas.

HOXTON. As wide as you like, you'll never——

> [WELLWYN *pushes* ANN *back into the house and
> closes the door behind her. The voices are still
> faintly heard arguing on the threshold.*

BERTLEY. Let me go in here a minute, Wellwyn. I must finish speaking to her. [*He motions* MRS. MEGAN *towards the model's room.*] We can't leave the matter thus.

FERRAND. [*Suavely.*] Do you desire my company, Monsieur?

> [BERTLEY, *with a prohibitive gesture of his hand,*
> *shepherds the reluctant* MRS. MEGAN *into the*
> *model's room.*

WELLWYN. [*Sorrowfully.*] You shouldn't have done this, Ferrand. It wasn't the square thing.

FERRAND. [*With dignity.*] Monsieur, I feel that I am in the wrong. It was stronger than me.

> [*As he speaks,* SIR THOMAS HOXTON *and* PRO-
> FESSOR CALWAY *enter from the house. In the*
> *dim light, and the full cry of argument, they do*
> *not notice the figures at the fire.* SIR THOMAS
> HOXTON *leads towards the street door.*

HOXTON. No, sir, I repeat, if the country once commits itself to your views of reform, it's as good as doomed.

CALWAY. I seem to have heard that before, Sir Thomas. And let me say at once that your hitty-missy cart-load of bricks *régime*——

HOXTON. Is a deuced sight better, sir, than your grand-motherly methods. What the old fellow wants is a shock! With all this socialistic molly-coddling, you're losing sight of the individual.

CALWAY. [*Swiftly.*] You, sir, with your "devil take the hindmost," have never even seen him.

> [SIR THOMAS HOXTON, *throwing back a gesture of*
> *disgust, steps out into the night, and falls heavily.*

PROFESSOR CALWAY, *hastening to his rescue, falls more heavily still.*

[TIMSON, *momentarily roused from slumber on the doorstep, sits up.*

HOXTON. [*Struggling to his knees.*] Damnation!

CALWAY. [*Sitting.*] How simultaneous!

[WELLWYN *and* FERRAND *approach hastily.*

FERRAND. [*Pointing to* TIMSON.] Monsieur, it was true, it seems. They had lost sight of the individual.

[*A Policeman has appeared under the street lamp. He picks up* HOXTON's *hat.*

CONSTABLE. Anything wrong, sir?

HOXTON. [*Recovering his feet.*] Wrong? Great Scott! Constable! Why do you let things lie about in the street like this? Look here, Wellwyn!

[*They all scrutinize* TIMSON.

WELLWYN. It's only the old fellow whose reform you were discussing.

HOXTON. How did he come here?

CONSTABLE. Drunk, sir. [*Ascertaining* TIMSON *to be in the street.*] Just off the premises, by good luck. Come along, father.

TIMSON. [*Assisted to his feet—drowsily.*] Cert'nly, by no means; take my arm.

[*They move from the doorway.* HOXTON *and* CALWAY *re-enter, and go towards the fire.*

ANN. [*Entering from the house.*] What's happened?

CALWAY. Might we have a brush?

HOXTON. [*Testily.*] Let it dry!

[*He moves to the fire and stands before it.* PRO-
FESSOR CALWAY *following stands a little behind
him.* ANN *returning begins to brush the* PRO-
FESSOR'S *sleeve.*

WELLWYN. [*Turning from the door, where he has stood
looking after the receding* TIMSON.] Poor old Timson!

FERRAND. [*Softly.*] Must be philosopher, Monsieur!
They will but run him in a little.

[*From the model's room* MRS. MEGAN *has come
out, shepherded by* CANON BERTLEY.

BERTLEY. Let's see, your Christian name is——.

MRS. MEGAN. Guinevere.

BERTLEY. Oh! Ah! Ah! Ann, take Gui—— take
our little friend into the study a minute: I am going to
put her into service. We shall make a new woman of
her, yet.

ANN. [*Handing* CANON BERTLEY *the brush, and turning to* MRS. MEGAN.] Come on!

[*She leads into the house, and* MRS. MEGAN *follows
stolidly.*

BERTLEY. [*Brushing* CALWAY'S *back.*] Have you
fallen?

CALWAY. Yes.

BERTLEY. Dear me! How was that?

HOXTON. That old ruffian dr nk on the doorstep.
Hope they'll give him a sharp dose! These rag-tags!

[*He looks round, and his angry eyes light by chance
on* FERRAND.

FERRAND. [*With his eyes on* HOXTON—*softly.*] Monsieur, something tells me it is time I took the road again.

WELLWYN. [*Fumbling out a sovereign.*] Take this, then!

FERRAND. [*Refusing the coin.*] Non, Monsieur. To abuse 'ospitality is not in my character.

BERTLEY. We must not despair of anyone.

HOXTON. Who talked of despairing? Treat him, as I say, and you'll see!

CALWAY. The interest of the State——

HOXTON. The interest of the individual citizen sir——

BERTLEY. Come! A little of both, a little of both!

> [*They resume their brushing.*

FERRAND. You are now debarrassed of us three, Monsieur. I leave you instead—these sirs. [*He points.*] *Au revoir, Monsieur!* [*Motioning towards the fire.*] 'Appy New Year!

> [*He slips quietly out.* WELLWYN, *turning, con-
> templates the three reformers. They are all now
> brushing away, scratching each other's backs,
> and gravely hissing. As he approaches them,
> they speak with a certain unanimity.*

HOXTON. My theory——!

CALWAY. My theory——!

BERTLEY. My theory——!

> [*They stop surprised.* WELLWYN *makes a gesture
> of discomfort, as they speak again with still more
> unanimity.*

HOXTON. My——!
CALWAY. My——!
BERTLEY. My——!

> [*They stop in greater surprise.*
> *The stage is blotted dark.*

Curtain.

ACT III

*It is the first of April—a white spring day of gleams and
driving showers. The street door of* WELLWYN'S
*studio stands wide open, and, past it, in the street,
the wind is whirling bits of straw and paper bags.
Through the door can be seen the butt end of a sta-
tionary furniture van with its flap let down. To this
van three humble-men in shirt sleeves and aprons,
are carrying out the contents of the studio. The hissing samovar, the tea-pot, the sugar, and the nearly
empty decanter of rum stand on the low round table
in the fast-being-gutted room.* WELLWYN *in his
ulster and soft hat, is squatting on the little stool in
front of the blazing fire, staring into it, and smoking
a hand-made cigarette. He has a moulting air.
Behind him the humble-men pass, embracing busts
and other articles of vertu.*

CHIEF H'MAN. [*Stopping, and standing in the attitude
of expectation.*] We've about pinched this little lot, sir.
Shall we take the—reservoir?

[*He indicates the samovar.*

WELLWYN. Ah! [*Abstractedly feeling in his pockets,
and finding coins.*] Thanks—thanks—heavy work, I'm
afraid.

59

H'MAN. [*Receiving the coins—a little surprised and a good deal pleased.*] Thank'ee, sir. Much obliged, I'm sure. We'll 'ave to come back for this. [*He gives the dais a vigorous push with his foot.*] Not a fixture, as I understand. Perhaps you'd like us to leave these 'ere for a bit.   [*He indicates the tea things.*

WELLWYN. Ah! do.

> [*The humble-men go out. There is the sound of horses being started, and the butt end of the van disappears. WELLWYN stays on his stool, smoking and brooding over the fire. The open doorway is darkened by a figure. CANON BERT-LEY is standing there.*

BERTLEY. Wellwyn! [WELLWYN *turns and rises.*] It's ages since I saw you. No idea you were moving. This is very dreadful.

WELLWYN. Yes, Ann found this—too exposed. That tall house in Flight Street—we're going there. Seventh floor.

BERTLEY. Lift?

> [WELLWYN *shakes his head.*

BERTLEY. Dear me! No lift? Fine view, no doubt. [WELLWYN *nods.*] You'll be greatly missed.

WELLWYN. So Ann thinks. Vicar, what's become of that little flower-seller I was painting at Christmas? You took her into service.

BERTLEY. Not we—exactly! Some dear friends of ours. Painful subject!

WELLWYN. Oh!

BERTLEY. Yes. She got the footman into trouble.

WELLWYN. Did she, now?

BERTLEY. Disappointing. I consulted with Calway, and he advised me to try a certain institution. We got her safely in—excellent place; but, d'you know, she broke out three weeks ago. And since—I've heard— [*he holds his hands up*] hopeless, I'm afraid—quite!

WELLWYN. I *thought* I saw her last night. You can't tell me her address, I suppose?

BERTLEY. [*Shaking his head.*] The husband too has quite passed out of my ken. He betted on horses, you remember. I'm sometimes tempted to believe there's nothing for some of these poor folk but to pray for death.

> [ANN *has entered from the house. Her hair hangs*
> *from under a knitted cap. She wears a white*
> *wool jersey, and a loose silk scarf.*

BERTLEY. Ah! Ann. I was telling your father of that poor little Mrs. Megan.

ANN. Is she dead?

BERTLEY. Worse I fear. By the way—what became of her accomplice?

ANN. We haven't seen him since. [*She looks searchingly at* WELLWYN.] At least—have *you*—Daddy?

WELLWYN. [*Rather hurt.*] No, my dear; I have not.

BERTLEY. And the—old gentleman who drank the rum?

ANN. He got fourteen days. It was the fifth time.

BERTLEY. Dear me!

ANN. When he came out he got more drunk than ever. Rather a score for Professor Calway, wasn't it?

BERTLEY. I remember. He and Sir Thomas took a kindly interest in the old fellow.

ANN. Yes, they fell over him. The Professor got him into an Institution.

BERTLEY. Indeed!

ANN. He was perfectly sober all the time he was there.

WELLWYN. My dear, they only allow them milk.

ANN. Well, anyway, he was reformed.

WELLWYN. Ye—yes!

ANN. [*Terribly.*] Daddy! You've been seeing him!

WELLWYN. [*With dignity.*] My dear, I have not.

ANN. How do you know, then?

WELLWYN. Came across Sir Thomas on the Embankment yesterday; told me old Timson had been had up again for sitting down in front of a brewer's dray.

ANN. Why?

WELLWYN. Well, you see, as soon as he came out of the what d'you call 'em, he got drunk for a week, and it left him in low spirits.

BERTLEY. Do you mean he deliberately sat down, with the intention—of—er?

WELLWYN. Said he was tired of life, but they didn't believe him.

ANN. Rather a score for Sir Thomas! I suppose he'd told the Professor? What did *he* say?

WELLWYN. Well, the Professor said [*with a quick glance at* BERTLEY] he felt there was nothing for some of these poor devils but a lethal chamber.

BERTLEY. [*Shocked.*] Did he really!

　　　　　[*He has not yet caught* WELLWYN'S *glance.*

WELLWYN. And Sir Thomas agreed. Historic occasion. And you, Vicar—H'm!

　　　　　　　　　　　　　[BERTLEY *winces.*

ANN. [*To herself.*] Well, there isn't.

BERTLEY. And yet! Some good in the old fellow, no doubt, if one could put one's finger on it. [*Preparing to go.*] You'll let us know, then, when you're settled. What was the address? [WELLWYN *takes out and hands him a card.*] Ah! yes. Good-bye, Ann. Good-bye, Wellwyn. [*The wind blows his hat along the street.*] What a wind!　　　　　　　　　[*He goes, pursuing.*

ANN. [*Who has eyed the card askance.*] Daddy, have you told those other two where we're going?

WELLWYN. Which other two, my dear?

ANN. The Professor and Sir Thomas.

WELLWYN. Well, Ann, naturally I——

ANN. [*Jumping on to the dais with disgust.*] Oh, dear! When I'm trying to get you away from all this atmosphere. I don't so much mind the Vicar knowing, because he's got a weak heart——

　　　　　　　　　　　　　[*She jumps off again.*

WELLWYN. [*To himself.*] Seventh floor! I felt there was something.

ANN. [*Preparing to go.*] I'm going round now. But you must stay here till the van comes back. And don't forget you tipped the men after the first load.

WELLWYN. Oh! yes, yes. [*Uneasily.*] Good sorts they look, those fellows!

ANN. [*Scrutinising him.*] What have you done?

WELLWYN. Nothing, my dear, really——!

ANN. What?

WELLWYN. I—I rather think I may have tipped them twice.

ANN. [*Drily.*] Daddy! If it *is* the first of April, it's not necessary to make a fool of *oneself*. That's the last time you ever do these ridiculous things. [WELLWYN *eyes her askance.*] I'm going to see that you spend your money on yourself. You needn't look at me like that! I *mean* to. As soon as I've got you away from here, and all—these——

WELLWYN. Don't rub it in, Ann!

ANN. [*Giving him a sudden hug—then going to the door—with a sort of triumph.*] Deeds, not words, Daddy!

> [*She goes out, and the wind catching her scarf blows it out beneath her firm young chin. WELLWYN returning to the fire, stands brooding, and gazing at his extinct cigarette.*

WELLWYN. [*To himself.*] Bad lot—low type! No method! No theory!

> [*In the open doorway appear FERRAND and MRS. MEGAN. They stand, unseen, looking at him. FERRAND is more ragged, if possible, than on Christmas Eve. His chin and cheeks are clothed in a reddish golden beard. MRS. MEGAN'S dress is not so woe-begone, but her face is white, her eyes dark-circled. They whisper. She slips back into the shadow of the doorway. WELL-*

WYN *turns at the sound, and stares at* FERRAND
in amazement.

FERRAND. [*Advancing.*] Enchanted to see you, Monsieur. [*He looks round the empty room.*] You are leaving?

WELLWYN. [*Nodding—then taking the young man's hand.*] How goes it?

FERRAND. [*Displaying himself, simply.*] As you see, Monsieur. I have done of my best. It still flies from me.

WELLWYN. [*Sadly—as if against his will.*] Ferrand, it will always fly.

[*The young foreigner shivers suddenly from head to foot; then controls himself with a great effort.*

FERRAND. Don't say that, Monsieur! It is too much the echo of my heart.

WELLWYN. Forgive me! I didn't mean to pain you.

FERRAND. [*Drawing nearer the fire.*] That old cabby, Monsieur, you remember—they tell me, he nearly succeeded to gain happiness the other day.

[WELLWYN *nods.*

FERRAND. And those Sirs, so interested in him, with their theories? He has worn them out? [WELLWYN *nods.*] That goes without saying. And now they wish for him the lethal chamber.

WELLWYN. [*Startled.*] How did you know that?

[*There is silence.*

FERRAND. [*Staring into the fire.*] Monsieur, while I was on the road this time I fell ill of a fever. It seemed to me in my illness that I saw the truth—how I was wasting in this world—I would never be good for any one—nor any one for me—all would go by, and I never of it—fame, and fortune, and peace, even the necessities of life, ever mocking me.

>   [*He draws closer to the fire, spreading his fingers
>   to the flame. And while he is speaking, through
>   the doorway* MRS. MEGAN *creeps in to listen.*

FERRAND. [*Speaking on into the fire.*] And I saw, Monsieur, so plain, that I should be vagabond all my days, and my days short, I dying in the end the death of a dog. I saw it all in my fever—clear as that flame —there was nothing for us others, but the herb of death. [WELLWYN *takes his arm and presses it.*] And so, Monsieur, I *wished* to die. I told no one of my fever. I lay out on the ground—it was verree cold. But they would not let me die on the roads of their parishes— they took me to an Institution, Monsieur, I looked in their eyes while I lay there, and I saw more clear than the blue heaven that they thought it best that I should die, although they would not let me. Then Monsieur, naturally my spirit rose, and I said: "So much the worse for you. I will live a little more." One is made like that! Life is sweet, Monsieur.

WELLWYN. Yes, Ferrand; Life is sweet.

FERRAND. That little girl you had here, Monsieur— [WELLWYN *nods.*] in her too there is something of wild-savage. She must have joy of life. I have seen her since I came back. She has embraced the life of joy. It is not quite the same thing. [*He lowers his voice.*] She is lost, Monsieur, as a stone that sinks in water. I can see, if she cannot. [*As* WELLWYN *makes a movement of distress.*] Oh! I am not to blame for that, Monsieur. It had well begun before I knew her.

WELLWYN. Yes, yes—I was afraid of it, at the time.

[MRS. MEGAN *turns silently, and slips away.*

FERRAND. I do my best for her, Monsieur, but look at me! Besides, I am not good for her—it is not good for simple souls to be with those who see things clear. For the great part of mankind, to see anything—is fatal.

WELLWYN. Even for you, it seems.

FERRAND. No, Monsieur. To be so near to death has done me good; I shall not lack courage any more till the wind blows on my grave. Since I saw you, Monsieur, I have been in three Institutions. They are palaces. One may eat upon the floor—though it is true—for Kings—they eat too much of skilly there. One little thing they lack—those palaces. It is under-standing of the 'uman heart. In them tame birds pluck wild birds naked.

WELLWYN. They mean well.

FERRAND. Ah! Monsieur, I am loafer, waster—what you like—for all that [*bitterly*] poverty is my only crime. If I were rich, should I not be simply veree original, 'ighly respected, with soul above commerce, travelling to see the world? And that young girl, would she not be "that charming ladee." "veree *chic*, you know!" And the old Tims—good old-fashioned gentleman—drinking his liquor well. *Eh! bien*—what are we now? Dark beasts, despised by all. That is life, Monsieur.   [*He stares into the fire.*

WELLWYN. We're our own enemies, Ferrand. I can afford it—you can't. Quite true!

FERRAND. [*Earnestly.*] Monsieur, do you know this? You are the sole being that can do us good—we hopeless ones.

WELLWYN. [*Shaking his head.*] Not a bit of it; I'm hopeless too.

FERRAND. [*Eagerly.*] Monsieur, it is just that. You *understand*. When we are with you we feel something —here—[*he touches his heart.*] If I had one prayer to make, it would be, Good God, give me to understand! Those sirs, with their theories, they can clean our skins and chain our 'abits—that soothes for them the æsthetic sense; it gives them too their good little importance. But our spirits they cannot touch, for they nevare understand. Without that, Monsieur, all is dry as a parched skin of orange.

WELLWYN. Don't be so bitter. Think of all the work they do!

FERRAND. Monsieur, of their industry I say nothing. They do a good work while they attend with their theories to the sick and the tame old, and the good unfortunate deserving. Above all to the little children. But, Monsieur, when all is done, there are always us hopeless ones. What can they do with me, Monsieur, with that girl, or with that old man? Ah! Monsieur, we, too, 'ave our qualities, we others—it wants you courage to undertake a career like mine, or like that young girl's. We wild ones—we know a thousand times more of life than ever will those sirs. They waste their time trying to make rooks white. Be kind to us if you will, or let us alone like Mees Ann, but do not try to change our skins. Leave us to live, or leave us to die when we like in the free air. If you do not wish of us, you have but to shut your pockets and your doors —we shall die the faster.

WELLWYN. [*With agitation.*] But that, you know— we can't do—now can we?

FERRAND. If you cannot, how is it our fault? The harm we do to others—is it so much? If I am criminal, dangerous—shut me up! I would not pity myself— nevare. But we in whom something moves—like that flame, Monsieur, that *cannot* keep still—we others— we are not many—that must have motion in our lives, do not let them make us prisoners, with their theories, because we are not like them—it is life itself they would enclose! [*He draws up his tattered figure, then bending over the fire again.*] I ask your pardon; I am talking. If I could smoke, Monsieur!

> [WELLWYN *hands him a tobacco pouch; and he rolls a cigarette with his yellow-stained fingers.*

FERRAND. The good God made me so that I would rather walk a whole month of nights, hungry, with the stars, than sit one single day making round busi- ness on an office stool! It is not to my advantage. I cannot help it that I am a vagabond. What would you have? It is stronger than me. [*He looks suddenly at* WELLWYN.] Monsieur, I say to you things I have never said.

WELLWYN. [*Quietly.*] Go on, go on. [*There is silence.*

FERRAND. [*Suddenly.*] Monsieur! Are you really English? The English are so civilised.

WELLWYN. And am I not?

FERRAND. You treat me like a brother.

> [WELLWYN *has turned towards the street door at a sound of feet, and the clamour of voices.*

TIMSON. [*From the street.*] Take her in 'ere. I knows 'im.

> [*Through the open doorway come a* POLICE CON-STABLE *and a* LOAFER, *bearing between them the limp white-faced form of* MRS. MEGAN, *hatless and with drowned hair, enveloped in the police-man's waterproof. Some curious persons bring up the rear, jostling in the doorway, among whom is* TIMSON *carrying in his hands the policeman's dripping waterproof leg pieces.*

FERRAND. [*Starting forward.*] Monsieur, it is that little girl!

WELLWYN. What's happened? Constable! What's happened!

> [*The* CONSTABLE *and* LOAFER *have laid the body down on the dais; with* WELLWYN *and* FER-RAND *they stand bending over her.*

CONSTABLE. 'Tempted sooicide, sir; but she hadn't been in the water 'arf a minute when I got hold of her. [*He bends lower.*] Can't understand her collapsin' like this.

WELLWYN. [*Feeling her heart.*] I don't feel anything.

FERRAND. [*In a voice sharpened by emotion.*] Let me try, Monsieur.

CONSTABLE. [*Touching his arm.*] You keep off, my lad.

WELLWYN. No, constable—let him.   He's her friend.

CONSTABLE. [*Releasing* FERRAND—*to the* LOAFER.] Here you!   Cut off for a doctor—sharp now!   [*He pushes back the curious persons.*] Now then, stand away there, please—we can't have you round the body.   Keep back—Clear out, now!

> [*He slowly moves them back, and at last shepherds them through the door and shuts it on them,* TIMSON *being last.*]

FERRAND. The rum!

> [WELLWYN *fetches the decanter.   With the little there is left* FERRAND *chafes the girl's hands and forehead, and pours some between her lips. But there is no response from the inert body.*]

FERRAND. Her soul is still away, Monsieur!

> [WELLWYN, *seizing the decanter, pours into it tea and boiling water.*]

CONSTABLE. It's never drownin', sir—her head was hardly under; I was on to her like knife.

FERRAND. [*Rubbing her feet.*] She has not yet her philosophy, Monsieur; at the beginning they often try. If she is dead! [*In a voice of awed rapture.*] What fortune!

CONSTABLE. [*With puzzled sadness.*] True enough, sir—that!   We'd just begun to know 'er.   If she 'as been taken—her best friends couldn't wish 'er better.

WELLWYN. [*Applying the decanter to her lips.*] Poor little thing!   I'll try this hot tea.

FERRAND. [*Whispering.*] *La mort—le grand ami!*

WELLWYN. Look! Look at her! She's coming round!

> [*A faint tremor passes over* MRS. MEGAN's *body. He again applies the hot drink to her mouth. She stirs and gulps.*

CONSTABLE. [*With intense relief.*] That's brave! Good lass! She'll pick up now, sir.

> [*Then, seeing that* TIMSON *and the curious persons have again opened the door, he drives them out, and stands with his back against it.* MRS. MEGAN *comes to herself.*

WELLWYN. [*Sitting on the dais and supporting her— as if to a child.*] There you are, my dear. There, there—better now! That's right. Drink a little more of this tea.

> [MRS. MEGAN *drinks from the decanter.*

FERRAND. [*Rising.*] Bring her to the fire, Monsieur.

> [*They take her to the fire and seat her on the little stool. From the moment of her restored animation* FERRAND *has resumed his air of cynical detachment, and now stands apart with arms folded, watching.*

WELLWYN. Feeling better, my child?

MRS. MEGAN. Yes.

WELLWYN. That's good. That's good. Now, how was it? Um?

MRS. MEGAN. I dunno. [*She shivers.*] I was standin' here just now when you was talkin', and when I heard 'im, it **cam'** over me to do it—like.

WELLWYN. Ah, yes *I* know.

MRS. MEGAN. I didn't seem no good to meself nor any one. But when I got in the water, I didn't want to any more. It was cold in there.

WELLWYN. Have you been having such a bad time of it?

MRS. MEGAN. Yes. And listenin' to him upset me. [*She signs with her head at* FERRAND.] I feel better now I've been in the water.   [*She smiles and shivers.*

WELLWYN. There, there! Shivery? Like to walk up and down a little?

              [*They begin walking together up and down.*

WELLWYN. Beastly when your head goes under?

MRS. MEGAN. Yes. It frightened me. I thought I wouldn't come up again.

WELLWYN. I know—sort of world without end, wasn't it? What did you think of, um?

MRS. MEGAN. I wished I 'adn't jumped—an' I thought of my baby—that died—and—[*in a rather surprised voice*] and I thought of d-dancin'.

      [*Her mouth quivers, her face puckers, she gives a
           choke and a little sob.*

WELLWYN. [*Stopping and stroking her.*] There, there —there!

      [*For a moment her face is buried in his sleeve, then
           she recovers herself.*

MRS. MEGAN. Then 'e got hold o' me, an' pulled me out.

WELLWYN. Ah! what a comfort—um?

MRS. MEGAN. Yes. The water got into me mouth.

[*They walk again.*] I wouldn't have gone to do it but for *him.* [*She looks towards* FERRAND.] His talk made me feel all funny, as if people wanted me to.

WELLWYN. My dear child! Don't think such things! As if anyone would——!

MRS. MEGAN. [*Stolidly.*] I thought they did. They used to look at me so sometimes, where I was before I ran away—I couldn't stop there, you know.

WELLWYN. Too cooped-up?

MRS. MEGAN. Yes. ,No life at all, it wasn't—not after sellin' flowers, I'd rather be doin' what I am.

WELLWYN. Ah! Well—it's all over, now! How d'you feel—eh? Better?

MRS. MEGAN. Yes. I feels all right now.

[*She sits up again on the little stool before the fire.*
WELLWYN. No shivers, and no aches; quite comfy?

MRS. MEGAN. Yes.

WELLWYN. That's a blessing. All well, now, Constable—-thank you!

CONSTABLE. [*Who has remained discreetly apart at the door—cordially.*] First rate, sir! That's capital! [*He approaches and scrutinises* MRS. MEGAN.] Right as rain, eh, my girl?

MRS. MEGAN. [*Shrinking a little.*] Yes.

CONSTABLE. That's fine. Then I think perhaps, for 'er sake, sir, the sooner we move on and get her a change o' clothin', the better.

WELLWYN. Oh! don't bother about that—I'll send round for my daughter—we'll manage for her here.

CONSTABLE. Very kind of you, I'm sure, sir. But [*with embarrassment*] she seems all right. She'll get every attention at the station.

WELLWYN. But I assure you, we don't mind at all; we'll take the greatest care of her.

CONSTABLE. [*Still more embarrassed.*] Well, sir, of course, I'm thinkin' of—— I'm afraid I can't depart from the usual course.

WELLWYN. [*Sharply.*] What! But—oh! No! No! That'll be all right, Constable! That'll be all right! I assure you.

CONSTABLE. [*With more decision.*] I'll have to charge her, sir.

WELLWYN. Good God! You don't mean to say the poor little thing has got to be——

CONSTABLE. [*Consulting with him.*] Well, sir, we can't get over the facts, can we? There it is! You know what sooicide amounts to—it's an awkward job.

WELLWYN. [*Calming himself with an effort.*] But look here, Constable, as a reasonable man—— This poor wretched little girl—*you* know what that life means better than anyone! Why! It's to her credit to try and jump out of it!

[*The* CONSTABLE *shakes his head.*

WELLWYN. You said yourself her best friends couldn't wish her better! [*Dropping his voice still more.*] Everybody feels it! The Vicar was here a few minutes ago saying the very same thing—the Vicar, Constable! [*The* CONSTABLE *shakes his head.*] Ah! now, look here, I know something of her. Nothing can be done with her. We all admit it. Don't you see? Well, then hang it—you needn't go and make fools of us all by——

FERRAND. Monsieur, it is the first of April.

CONSTABLE. [*With a sharp glance at him.*] Can't neglect me duty, sir; that's impossible.

WELLWYN. Look here! She—slipped. She's been telling me. Come, Constable, there's a good fellow. May be the making of her, this.

CONSTABLE. I quite appreciate your good 'eart, sir, an' you make it very 'ard for me—but, come now! I put it to you as a gentleman, would you go back on yer duty if you was me?

> [WELLWYN *raises his hat, and plunges his fingers through and through his hair.*

WELLWYN. Well! God in heaven! **Of** all the d——d topsy-turvy——! Not a soul in the world wants her alive—and now she's to be prosecuted for trying to be where everyone wishes her.

CONSTABLE. Come, sir, come! Be a man!

> [*Throughout all this* MRS. MEGAN *has sat stolidly before the fire, but as* FERRAND *suddenly steps forward she looks up at him.*

FERRAND. Do not grieve, Monsieur! This will give her courage. There is nothing that gives more courage than to see the irony of things. [*He touches* MRS. MEGAN's *shoulder.*] Go, my child; it will do you good.

> [MRS. MEGAN *rises, and looks at him dazedly.*

CONSTABLE. [*Coming forward, and taking her by the hand.*] That's my good lass. Come along! We won't hurt you.

MRS. MEGAN. I don't want to go.   They'll stare at me.

CONSTABLE. [*Comforting.*] Not they! I'll see to that.

WELLWYN. [*Very upset.*] Take her in a cab, Constable, if you must—for God's sake! [*He pulls out a shilling.*] Here!

CONSTABLE. [*Taking the shilling.*] I will, sir, certainly.   Don't think I want to——

WELLWYN. No, no, I know. You're a good sort.

CONSTABLE. [*Comfortable.*] Don't you take on, sir. It's her first try; they won't be hard on 'er. Like as not only bind 'er over in her own recogs not to do it again. Come, my dear.

MRS. MEGAN. [*Trying to free herself from the policeman's cloak.*] I want to take this off.   It looks so funny.

> [*As she speaks the door is opened by* ANN; *behind whom is dimly seen the form of old* TIMSON, *still heading the curious persons.*

ANN. [*Looking from one to the other in amaze.*] What is it? What's happened? Daddy!

FERRAND. [*Out of the silence.*] It is nothing, Ma'moiselle! She has failed to drown herself. They run her in a little.

WELLWYN. Lend her your jacket, my dear; she'll catch her death.

> [ANN, *feeling* MRS. MEGAN's *arm, strips off her jacket, and helps her into it without a word.*

CONSTABLE. [*Donning his cloak.*] Thank you, Miss— very good of you, I'm sure.

MRS. MEGAN. [*Mazed.*] It's warm!

> [*She gives them all a last half-smiling look, and passes with the* CONSTABLE *through the doorway.*

FERRAND. That makes the third of us, Monsieur. We are not in luck.   To wish us dead, it seems, is easier than to let us die.

> [*He looks at* ANN, *who is standing with her eyes fixed on her father.* WELLWYN *has taken from his pocket a visiting card.*

WELLWYN. [*To* FERRAND.] Here quick; take this, run after her!   When they've done with her tell her to come to us.

FERRAND. [*Taking the card, and reading the address.*] "No. 7, Haven House, Flight Street!"   Rely on me, Monsieur—I will bring her myself to call on you.   *Au revoir, mon bon Monsieur!*

> [*He bends over* WELLWYN'S *hand; then, with a bow to* ANN *goes out; his tattered figure can be seen through the window, passing in the wind.* WELLWYN *turns back to the fire.   The figure of* TIMSON *advances into the doorway, no longer holding in either hand a waterproof leg-piece.*

TIMSON. [*In a croaky voice.*] Sir!

WELLWYN. What—you, Timson?

TIMSON. On me larst legs, sir.   'Ere!   You can see 'em for yerself!   Shawn't trouble yer long.

WELLWYN. [*After a long and desperate stare.*] Not now—Timson—not now!   Take this! [*He takes out another card, and hands it to* TIMSON.] Some other time.

TIMSON. [*Taking the card.*] Yer new address! You *are* a gen'leman.   [*He lurches slowly away.*

> [ANN *shuts the street door and sets her back against it. The rumble of the approaching van is heard outside. It ceases.*

ANN. [*In a fateful voice.*] Daddy! [*They stare at each other.*] Do you know what you've done? Given your card to those six rotters.

WELLWYN. [*With a blank stare.*] Six?

ANN. [*Staring round the naked room.*] What was the good of this?

WELLWYN. [*Following her eyes—very gravely.*] Ann! It is stronger than me.

> [*Without a word* ANN *opens the door, and walks straight out. With a heavy sigh,* WELLWYN *sinks down on the little stool before the fire. The three humble-men come in.*

CHIEF HUMBLE-MAN. [*In an attitude of expectation.*] This is the larst of it, sir.

WELLWYN. Oh! Ah! yes!

> [*He gives them money; then something seems to strike him, and he exhibits certain signs of vexation. Suddenly he recovers, looks from one to the other, and then at the tea things. A faint smile comes on his face.*

WELLWYN. You can finish the decanter.

>   [*He goes out in haste.*

CHIEF HUMBLE-MAN. [*Clinking the coins.*] Third time of arskin'! April fool! Not 'arf! Good old pigeon!

Second Humble-Man. 'Uman being, *I* call 'im.

Chief Humble-Man. [*Taking the three glasses from the last packing-case, and pouring very equally into them.*] That's right.   Tell you wot, I'd never 'a touched this unless 'e'd told me to, I wouldn't—not with 'im.

Second Humble-Man. Ditto to that!   This is a bit of orl right! [*Raising his glass.*] Good luck!

Third Humble-Man. Same 'ere!

> [*Simultaneously they place their lips smartly against the liquor, and at once let fall their faces and their glasses.*

Chief Humble-Man. [*With great solemnity.*] Crikey! Bill!   *Tea!* . . .   'E's *got* us!

The stage is blotted dark.

Curtain.